Praise

"Brilliant. Beautiful. Chilling." —*A.S., Portland, OR*

"This shimmers in the distance, it gets in your face. It convulses and lies still and gasps again. I am not surprised at the fount of beauty, but in awe. . . . The words, the experience, the bravery . . . reading this feels like being loved with ferocity and tenderness."
—*M.W., Portland, Oregon*

"Is it possible for a piece of writing to be achingly painful and simultaneously luscious? I think I just read the answer." —*L.R., Victoria, British Columbia*

"Oh, how stories shape us . . . and when told, shape others'. [The author's] courage is stunningly beautiful. And my story is different today because of [hers]." —*R.D., Seattle, Washington*

"What a gift . . . as in talent, but more so a generous offering. There are so many lines, thoughts, even a single choice of a word that make me stop and reflect. They make me feel good and safe. Like this line: "carrying this body-density and this spirit-clarity." It makes me want to have a good cry just to feel that. It's so palpable." —*B.P., New York, New York*

"Brave and generous. Brings total strangers together so we can see that we are not alone. The world is a better place because of it."
—*L.S., Minneapolis, Minnesota*

"Left me full of wonder. Told with such purity and freedom. [The author's] capacity as a conduit for healing . . . a manifestation of Grace." —*N.L., Camas, Washington*

"WOW . . . writing [that] jumps off the pages; visuals that are so easy to digest. This, specifically: "Grief waters the flower to bloom again and again and again." —*K.F., Boston, Massachusetts*

"This book really helped me in terms of facing some of the grief and the whole (waves hands at the world) crazy life/soul journey." —*L.S., Santa Barbara, California*

"Incredible. This one could crack open the world." —*S.D.H., Portland, Oregon*

"Beautiful and hard and honest and needed." —*A.B.S., Ventura, California*

"Wow. I am calmed and comforted and grateful." —*D.L., Portland, Oregon*

"Transfixed." —*S.B., San Francisco, California*

"Speechless." —*G.B., Vancouver, British Columbia*

"This work is sacred." —*C.L., Houston, Texas*

ASH
AND
SPIRIT

ASH
AND
SPIRIT

**Freeing Grief and Finding Hope
in 31 Days of Memories, Mediumship,
and Collective Healing**

PEMA ROCKER

7th Mind
Publishing

7th Mind
Publishing

Expanded print edition published September 2024
Original ebook published September 2021
7th Mind Publishing
Santa Barbara, California

Editor: Jenefer Angell
Cover design: Wanna Johansson
Ebook design: Ellie Sipila
Print design: Morgan Krehbiel

For speaking engagements please email hello@storycharmer.com.

ISBN: 978-1-7365898-8-5 (print)
ISBN: 978-1-7365898-9-2 (ebook)

In memory of those we lost, in honor of all who
lost a part of themselves, in eternal listening
for any who grieve anew and still. May we heal
together in our common bond.

For Suzy Schutz

Schutz, *German to English:*
safeguard, shelter, protector, refuge

Your loved ones are always here with you, just as the stars are. Stars do not "come out" at night, they are revealed. Reveal the presence of your loved ones in spirit by acknowledging that as points of consciousness in one unified field of consciousness, they cannot be anywhere but here.

—SANAYA

CONTENTS

PROLOGUE: ADRIFT

One night, I stood at the window in a friend's darkened bedroom, lights and voices ablaze past the living room wall. In my new city, I was wired and tired after the day that had gone down. I looked into a blue night, engulfed by it, and held the phone to my ear. It was my father on the other end. He was proud: I was alive. I had made it home.

His voice was curious awe, anchored like a dispatcher's calling from time eternal. My dad, long-ago adventurer, had rooted himself to a spot, dispatched me into this world, and listened while I reported my view, this time from a New York City street corner while the World Trade Center burned.

We didn't talk about feelings. We didn't cry about my graduate school classmates whose dorms were so close to the site they may still be trapped there, or contemplate how others may have got home that night, through the melting stench in the air so noxious new fear wafted with it each time the breeze shifted. He wanted to be where I was. Where the action was. Where history unfolded. To him, in his anchored life, I lived wishes.

I felt adult and childlike at once. On the phone with my father, I remembered thoughts that had plagued me earlier that morning: I had been calculating how many people died from the first plane's impact and, more to the point, how many people would open their doors that night to a coroner carrying news that their loved one was dead.

How many times had I remembered the coroner who came to our house? Her messy, blond curls. The run in her ivory-colored stockings. The silent cop by her side. And the view into the living room, my tall dad in my mom's teal robe—grabbed in haste on the way out of bed—hearing that his son was gone. My brother.

That may have been the day my anchor lifted, and my father's dropped. That's only a guess. I'll let him tell his own story. In my story, it's where the drift began, far, far away to an island where I could hear but couldn't speak. My internal world set up an ocean between it and the nearest dry land. Miles apart and the water wide, it would take a very long journey to return.

INTRODUCTION

When I stood on a New York City street corner on the morning of September 11, 2001, I was part of a city of eight million people watching its two tallest buildings disintegrate in an attack. We witnessed the deaths of over 2,600 people in those towers, and watched the city come to a halt. But on that day, as I struggled through confusion and shock and disbelief, along with everyone else I met along the long journey to get home, what I felt most viscerally were the traumas that had come before in my life.

In response to this wildly unfamiliar loss event, my brain opened up old memories, trying to find a reference point to understand the current trauma. It was like hearing a new song on the radio and your brain searching your memory to compare who that band sounds like so you can describe them to your friends. When the brain searches an emotional landscape for references for trauma, and wakes up every past loss it finds, it's post-traumatic stress in action.

Feeling the trauma in volume, it occurred to me, if I am one person in a city of millions whose past traumas are yawning open in the middle of grappling with the present one, what is going to become of us? How are we going to deal with this together?

In New York City, we had three days of shocked stillness. Not a horn honked. On the fourth day, people started to resume their habits and the streets filled again with people and traffic. Shrines of missing persons fliers and flowers and candles and hand-drawn poster boards filled the city's central squares and parks. But in time, those faded, post 9/11 life began, and for years to come, I gravitated toward rituals that would help us honor collective grief, collected grief, together.

I wanted the collective to grieve around me. I didn't know at the time that this desire stemmed from a lack of skill to grieve on my own. My family model for grieving to this point was a denial of feelings and a stoic drive to muscle on. After this massive trauma event, I needed to *see my need to grieve* mirrored in those around me. My feelings were raw, even though I had not experienced direct loss on 9/11. In comparison to others who had lost much more that day, I could barely acknowledge my peripheral losses let alone understand how to care for them in the context of a national attack. But still I felt hollow and lost. I craved the collective to show me what to do, and give me a kind of permission to feel. I went to stage plays and movies, appreciated artists processing the attacks. I read articles. But soon those waned, life carried on, and the collective focused away from trauma.

It's fascinating how life serves up its lessons. Read: You can't always get what you want, but you get what you need. In the years that followed 9/11/01, I dropped out of grad school; lived on fifty dollars a week; lost months of memory focusing only on where the next meal would come from; felt the edges of a terrifying depression; feared that, without support, my mental health would worsen and remain shaky for the rest of my life; and lived on the heartfelt charity of old friends and people I had just met. Meanwhile, I was training for a half-marathon (my daily sanity relying on the endorphin supply), slinging my ambition in Hollywood temp jobs while trying to get paid for my work, and online dating, trying to locate myself in relationship to others. I had no idea the hard times I had fallen on related to unexpressed grief. I powered through, wondering what happened to the happy person I used to be.

One day, in a new job, in the town where friends caught me after my Hollywood fall, construction noises came into the office from three sides of the building—jack hammer on pavement, workers yelling to be heard over nail guns on wood, tractor noises rumbling beneath the windows. My breath got heavy and my heart thudded. I couldn't process what my co-worker was asking me. My skin turned a clammy pall but I sweated through my blouse. I don't remember leaving but I found myself at home in my front yard, calling my friend who was studying to become a psychotherapist. She told me I was having a panic attack, and that I needed to put my hands in the grass and focus on my breathing. Between centering breaths, I thought about my new, constant desire to tell my colleagues to F-off—inhaled—and this new, terrifying feeling of being out of control—exhaled. And then I chalked it up to stress on the job.

A week later, the massage therapist I booked in response to my panic attack moved my limbs around and asked me questions:

"Wow, you're tight. Have you never had a massage?"

"Would you say your level of stress has increased recently?"

"Oh, you were in New York on 9/11? Have you checked to see if you have souls in your field?"

Record scratch. "What in my what?"

A metaphysical curveball

It was too much for me to swallow but months later her question still haunted me. By this time, however, my attention was consumed by a full-body psoriasis flare up like I had never seen, covered in red, itching, scaling skin, from collar bones to toes. At lunchtime, I'd go home from work to put on oil and lie in stillness for a half hour. At the end of the work day, I'd be in itchy, anxious pain all over again and go home to a medicinal bath. Three months in, after dermatologists and UV light treatments and an elimination diet that eliminated so much, I lost twenty pounds, I was still in agony and willing to try anything. Creams, tonics, colonics, hypnotherapy, energy therapy, somatics—thanking stars all the way that I had a job to pay for it. Finally, I tried Robin, a psychic medium I had met and vetted for weeks before asking her about my skin. She described my aura as porous and gave me some meditations to do. I shrugged, did them, bathed in saltwater, and said the prayers she taught me. In two weeks' time, my skin didn't change, but my anxiety came down. I went to work calm and interacted with people less reactively. My worry about my skin morphed into sadness. I felt sad and tired and I wanted to be held. I took medicinal baths with more patience, and sat in the meditations with more willingness.

It occurred to me to ask Robin the question about souls in my field. It took some weeks to build courage to call her. Still feeling skeptical, I kind of stuttered as I asked, but almost before I had even finished, she breathlessly said yes and began telling me what they were saying.

Her answer stunned me into stillness. As she continued, I felt a sensation in my body, as if my head opened at the top and my feet opened at the bottom and light shot through me in a gushing stream. I was sitting in my car when I called her, to get some privacy from my roommates on a Saturday morning. During the call, I opened my car door and stood up outside to get some air, move my body, feel my realness in this surreal moment. She started talking about the souls' bodies, how they grieved the loss of them. Surprised as I was with her rapid pace, and maintaining suspicion about what she was telling me, my head felt clear. Tears came. She asked me how I was doing. When I told her it was a lot to take in, she said the souls came to me because they knew I would be public about my experience with them.

The call ended. I walked around for two days with that physical feeling of light running from my head through my feet. Anxiety was gone. I felt happy and at ease. I recognized myself again.

Back at work, anxiety threatened and my sadness about the psoriasis crept back, but neither as heavily as before. I had felt something different and I wanted to know more. I wanted to understand. Most of all, if any of it was true, or even if it was a weird fantasy, here was a different kind of collective that was expressing its grief—through me!—for the same event that had affected us all and had shaken loose my historical losses a few years before.

I called Robin. I told her how I was feeling. I told her I wanted to live up to the souls saying they came to me because I would be public with their message. I asked her to channel them, so I could record what they shared through her, through me, and put it in a book so that any who wanted to could receive their messages and their deaths would not be in vain. Robin agreed.

On the day of our fourth session, the project took a turn. It was time for me to take my own spiritual journey into mediumship, the souls said. Here was the end of the idea, surely. I had swayed between my skepticism and my awe at the messages coming through; as much as I had come to believe someone else could be a channel for this material, I was certain that I could not be. But I also couldn't let go of the mystery.

Due to my own shame at not being ready to come out of the spiritual closet, when I told people about what I was writing, I told them the easier narrative that I was writing about collective grief after 9/11. And so it was in that direction the idea expanded: I began returning to New York on research trips to interview people who were present that day, visit memorials, learn people's stories, and journal my experiences.

The effect of these research trips and writing was a years-long exploration of my grief after 9/11. And in a bit of a bait and switch, a book never got off the ground. I researched and wrote and collaborated between 2005 and 2008, and by 2009, I had all but abandoned it. My life was taking off in a new direction in a new city with new, paid (finally!) work as a writer. I developed a long-term psychotherapy relationship, in which we excavated grief each visit. The psoriasis found the right combination of therapies to stabilize. In 2011, I found myself a few months from the tenth anniversary of 9/11, confronted by the fact that I hadn't done right by the souls who came to my field, or by the people I had spent those years interviewing, or by the still-thrumming desire to acknowledge grief in a collective experience. I hadn't written a book. It had been ten years. I had to do something.

Ten-year anniversary collective grief rite

Approaching September 11, 2011, I created my own grief rite for the collective, and for myself. Years of interviews and conversations had shown me a pattern; mine was not the only life that had been challenged in an ongoing way after witnessing the 9/11 World Trade Center attacks. Effects of the trauma were unfolding in different ways in each of our lives, from panic attacks to career failures to relationship endings. As we got closer, I noticed that ten-years-after was bringing up challenging memories again. In public observance of the anniversary, in memory of the people who died and the people they left behind, in observation of acknowledging grief in an individual and public way, and in an attempt to share what I learned about grief and loss through the souls that came to me all those years ago, I started a thirty-one-day grief writing journey on my blog, *Story Charmer*, and called it "Memory to Light."

I conceived of it as an interactive project that invited readers to witness my exploration of grief in the collective. I wrote a story a day and asked readers to write their memories in the comments, or to share about grief on their own blogs and link to my project. The result was a community that swelled with readers and tellers as we followed the narrative arc that my memories of loss were unfolding. Every day I wrote a memory triggered by something that had gone away, or someone I had lost. A vacant feeling, a desolate place, I gave it a space in story. I gave my emotions room to breathe. I let loss come to life instead of keeping it quiet because it hurt, and I invited others to remember their losses out loud with me. My thirty-one days of stories became the core of this book, complete with participants' memories and stories, shared in "Collective's voice" sections throughout.

A global collective loss to grieve

Deep into a pandemic, society is once again upended by an onslaught of grief. Our losses are personal, painful, confusing and ongoing, as separation, isolation, and recurring surges of the virus inhibit our efforts to quell the chaos, and challenge our mental health.

How do we cope with loss we are experiencing, alone and together? How do we grieve our individual traumas—trying to bury our dead, keep our livelihoods afloat, and soothe re-triggered hurts while keeping our families and ourselves well? And how do we grieve collectively, when this trauma is happening to all of us at the same time? How do we cope with loss of this magnitude?

This collective trauma, unlike many that have come before

it in our modern age—all the world's wars; the HIV/AIDS epidemic; Hurricanes Katrina and Maria; George Floyd's public murder by a police officer, its peak significance laid bare by subsequent international uprisings, everyday misogyny, bigotry, racism, and poverty that exhausted millions steel themselves against—this collective trauma of the pandemic has actively and consciously affected everyone around the globe.

We are made sensitive and tender. While preparing this text, written as an ebook in 2021, for its first printing in 2024, the global trauma keeps coming in waves. New wars, collateral human loss mounting to genocide in multiple countries, entrenched divisiveness—all drown out (while proliferating) a keening heartbreak. We went through a pandemic globally. We're attuned to a global awareness. Dare I say it's possible we feel each other more than we felt before? Compassion and contempt are delivered equally, all as the collective searches for self in a rubble of consequence. Traumas have so persisted, there has been little time to recover from the breakdowns that happen in their wake. There has been little time to find meaning, reconnection.

The mind boggles, and takes the opportunity for a more surgical slice at the earlier question, "Can we grieve collectively?" My questions now are: How *does* one grieve? Is it physical? Is it learned? Is it a language? Can we expect everyone to know how to actively acknowledge loss, recognize what their body needs to move through, trust it as it takes them over its aching path? Is it a skill to allow another's feelings when we're in the presence of their grief?

These years later, after therapy, body work, coaching, spiritual counsel; after marriage and divorce; 12-step recovery for dysfunctional family systems and codependence; through sacred self-storying; writing in dear groups of individuals exploring their own grief journeys, voicing trauma and putting loss to words, art-making mourning; and through consistent losses of loved ones, what I have barely just come to understand is that grief makes us part of the web of humanity. In grief we plummet, plunge, submerge, disappear. In acknowledging it, we let the voice of inner healing come nearer.

In putting this book together, my therapist pointed out that my urge and action to communally grieve spoke to an original wound of my family's, that of not being able to sufficiently express grief over a terrible early loss. In reaching out to others to witness my grief as I shared it in this project, and asking them to share theirs, too, I was recreating a family system that could hear and echo, share and feel all the sadness and anger and confusion. I did not know to do this before I started, I only knew that my practice of pulling together people to tell stories had felt good in the past, and maybe it would feel good to do it with an intention toward facing grief.

My therapist has a name for this action. The "emotional

immune system" is what she calls the part of ourselves that reaches out before we know what it means to reach out, and the urge I felt to hear and tell stories. She told me, "Your natural, organic ability to heal stepped in and allowed space for the grief. We all have a physical immune system. We have a natural ability to heal from emotional wounds, too. Much like our immune system works without us ever thinking about it—a cut will heal without you having to understand, intellectually, its healing—the emotional system has a natural desire to return to health and you don't have to understand it intellectually for it to work."

I thought about the times I just knew things without learning them. My body pulsed with understanding, remembering the many times in the course of my life that an intuition or an urge I couldn't explain took care of me, looked out for me, started me in the right direction. One of the times was at the end of my first year of grad school, when I heard a deeply buried but insistent inner voice urging me leave New York City and find shelter back home in the West because I would soon need the help of my friends. When I told my therapist, she said, "You can call it a spiritual center if you want. It's something beyond Self that is always there but we don't connect to it all the time because we are not practiced at listening for that voice inside us. When we start to listen to it, we start to connect with all of the parts of ourselves. We are not always tuned to that inner voice, but sometimes we are so desperate, we will listen to it. Part of our journey is to listen to it more and more, to get that deep self-knowing integrated, so that all of the different parts of our 'inner-self' become active in the immunity of our emotional system."

My emotional immune system taught me how I needed to grieve. My grieving connected me to other humans, and to the stronger natures within myself. In learning to connect with others, I learned more deeply to caretake myself in new ways, which in turn made me more available to hear and hold and help others when there is a need.

Humans connect. Reaching out to grieve together is a human thing to do. Right now, people are craving meaning and connection, seeking relief and purpose. Let's learn how we each grieve, and how we can link in our grief. Let's allow skill to build, to be there in compassion and understanding for ourselves and each other—through anger and heat, sorrow and loss. Let's remember that grief connects us to each other, and to the web of humanity.

What you'll find in this book, and how to read it

Ash and Spirit is a narrative collage told in nonlinear memories and constructed of interviews, messaging chats, journal entries, pictures, poems, and personal stories that take place over thirty years. *Ash and Spirit,* in its temporally agile form, represents the dislocated nature of memory and trauma recall. Vivid and detailed moments in time stitch together to tell a whole story of many losses into one for the sake of healing individual and collective grief.

Built on thirty-one days of storytelling, each "chapter" presents a new memory or picture or conversation excavating grief. Told together, the stories braid three narratives: The initial experience of a family tragedy laces through a second story fourteen years later from a New York City street corner on September 11, 2001. A third related story grapples with a health crisis that turns metaphysical in its resolution. The three stories weave together in witness, revelation, surprise, and release. Read from beginning to end to follow the narrative arcs. Or flip and read as your eye leads, to touch into a memory or story that has universal reach.

Throughout, the stories deliver healing through witness. "Collective's voice" sections represent community witness in its original presence on the 2011 daily blog series. The book includes topics addressing

- searching to understand grief
- processing grief through storytelling
- post-traumatic stress
- depression and mental health
- a physical health crisis
- considering grief as a skill

- early loss
- collective loss in family and community
- community participation in storytelling
- bearing witness
- connection to spirits of loved ones and others after they have died
- recovery and healing, and
- 9/11 attacks on the US.

The memories are potent. The stories are time capsules. The acknowledgement of grief is cleansing, and the presence of a community in the process is encouraging. As a result, the stories get delivered like medicine vials.

Emotional immune systems: activate

I'm not a grief counselor but I hope my work empowers you to find the support you need to traverse your own grief journey. Learning that I had grief to face, intentionally entering into the grief to acknowledge it, and later, learning skills to go even deeper and come out okay—that has all been really hard. But it hasn't been as hard or taken as long as my life before, in the time of desolation and unexpressed grief.

A note about finding support: resources are not easy to come by for everyone. This is the time to get what support we can, and find resource in each other as we grieve; turn toward each other and listen, turn toward each other and share.

I hope that, in the realm of silver linings—if there is a silver lining to a pandemic twenty years after the collective grief experience of 9/11—the loss that sickness and death has leveled at us, and the grief we have faced in isolation, will give us a way, a need, an inroad, to connect us to ourselves. I hope it will activate our emotional immune systems. And that, as this paves a path to connecting with others, we recognize connection, our need for it, how to do it, and that we relate to one another in this most human of urges.

I hope that this connection to our emotional immune system, inner voice, and intuition, can help us notice when and how to help ourselves, and others. How to keep the web connecting. And how, by tending to ourselves and each other in this way, we can develop a systemic immune system.

My hope for sharing this journey is to expose a human core in loss. Witnessing grief in each other softens us—if we are available to that: it's important to know it's not always true for everybody. But grief is an equalizer. It hits us all. If we can allow it, grief eventually helps us relate, experience empathy, build community, and feel belonging. May *Ash and Spirit* bring healing to your grief.

DAY 1
August 11, 2011

The idea

A story.

A day.

A story a day.

Mined from memory.

Framed by loss.

For the purpose of unearthing what's in there.

Remembering what has been.

Honoring it if it is there to be honored.

A remembrance

On September 11, 2001, my proximity to the World Trade Center attacks in New York City opened personal traumas I had neatly closed up and long since left behind.

For thirty-one days, I'll explore personal loss and collective grief in stories. I hope that as you read, you remember and share your stories in this collective forum, or write them down, or call a friend and remember out loud, in a spirit of connection and witness.

Witness

We want to be seen. Don't we? As humans in our experience? Acknowledged, understood. Is it possible that memories do too?

We are permeable. Grief moves into us. Inhabits us. If circumstances allow, it can move through us, if we're ready, if there's support, internal, systemic. If we can't let it move, grief can get as trapped in us as we get trapped in it. Sometimes it just . . . stays . . . till it's done with us.

Writing can bring circulation back to moments that have gone numb in us. With this thirty-one days, I want to breathe into memories that are rusted shut, and let them live, as vital figures. Honor the time and presence they've served in my life. I experienced them. I am whole. I was hobbled by not sharing them. Here, I am setting them free.

Fear

My fear is this: Who wants to hear about grief? Worse, who wants to mine for their own? Get close enough feel it? We are a distracted lot, posting and buying our fixes in the Twittermall, driving our cars to the next place. And then the next. Grief is allowed in our Western culture for a short, short time. But it lives on and on. If we bury it, grief under cover gestates. It begins to rule our lives in sideways attempts at escaping. But if we air it out and let it move, if there's room and support, we can weave it into our tapestry with the rest of our experiences, let it unravel and reshape, wilt and soften our humanness. Grief tenderizes. If we make it through, it offers us a willingness and skill to relate.

Grief is transformation

This exercise does not set out to be painful. Sometimes the exercise of grief is just a witnessing of what once was. A sound. A place. An idea. Once you give it witness you can let it transmute it into what it wants to become next, let it move on.

That said, there's inevitable pain in loss. Sometimes, you need a whole care team and a lot of time to help you through.

Giving space to grief, we become different than we were before. If we can make it, we reach another side of ourselves. We become stronger, more supple individuals, in a stronger, more supple collective—family, community, neighborhood, and hopefully, country.

Memory to light

Tell it. Release it—in small parts or big. Story is transformation. As readers we move through a catharsis with the storyteller. In their change, we are changed. Read with me, write with me, change with me.

DAY 2
Sweet Sixteen

I'm pretty sure my father held me when I was born, first time in his arms and said, "Beautiful. A healthy girl. You won't date till you're sixteen."

Whenever was the first time he said it, he wasn't kidding. Parties were off limits, too. He'd say, "If it's a boy who called, to you it's a party, to him it's a date."

In full teenage fury I'd throw back, "So he's dating *everybody there*? It's his BIRTHDAY PARTY!"

He'd say, "Don't argue."

As I got older, this rule grew more difficult to abide. Two years into high school, my social life was pastoral compared to most. The rule seemed particularly Draconian in springtime, when the end of school was in the air, and people had pool parties and all kinds of reasons to get together.

I got close once. From the time I could remember being a girl in company of boys, I had a secret crush on my brother's best friend from church. He was my friend too. He was in my grade. He called me up to ask me to a concert he was going to with my brother and his brother. It was set! We'd all go together. I had to call him back later to tell him I had to babysit. I couldn't go. My parents were going out, and I was staying home with my nine-year-old impairment of a little brother. I would have married that guy at twenty had I gone to that concert.

The days ticked by slowly. As spring set in and then summer leading up to my birthday, the arguments got fiercer. Sweet Sixteen was so close it seemed a technicality. Surely Dad would relent, if not for a one-on-one date then a group of kids hanging out, or a birthday party where parents were in-house.

"What?" I would plead after another invitation I'd had to turn down, "I'm gonna grow up all in the one night before I turn sixteen? Auugh!"

Turn of the heel. Flip of the hair. March from the room. His principle was crippling the point. He raised us to be mature beyond reason. His mantra for everything was, "Be wise."

My boy

When I say "us," I'm talking about my brother, David, a year older, our birthdays three days apart. Before I could pronounce his name as a little girl, I called him "my boy." Now we went to high school together. We were taking the same summer school class, both of us having failed algebra the first time around. That's right. All the wisdom in the world would not help "x" or "y" sort themselves out in an exam equation.

It was the night before my sixteenth. I was serene because I could see my future crackling open. I settled in to paint my toenails and get as cute as possible. I could date, like, tomorrow. It was going to be a full night of primping. David left the house with his buddies. His curfew had been extended two nights before on his birthday. Independence as a birthday present. Mine was on its way.

Hairpin

Close to midnight, the phone rings. I get to it first. It is the mom of David's friend, asking if we've received a call from the hospital. Through a haze of sleep, I hang the yellow receiver on the wall and tell my dad what she has said. Something about . . . an accident . . . they're okay . . . they can't tell us much more . . . but have we gotten a call? Do we have more information?

We haven't gotten a call. But they are okay. So that makes everything okay. Okay? We sleepwalk to our opposite parts of the house, back to bed. I wake up the minute I lay down, suddenly aware of the transaction I'd had on the phone.

In a half hour I see a red light revolving through the sheer curtain into my room. Then a knock at the door. I run to my dad's bedroom, heart pounding out of my eyeballs, panting, "There's someone here." Gawky limbs poke into in a too-small robe, knees and legs plunge through the dark to the living room. Dad answers the door in this state, in Mom's bright robe, me standing behind a ways, in the doorway leading to the room.

The end, the beginning

It's weird to me how, in trauma, what becomes clearest in that moment are the details. Color. Quiet. Angles. Breath.

I will tell you someday the details. But for the purpose of this story, two people step into the room. A woman, coroner. A man, cop. He confirms my father's name. Confirms that David Teeter is his son. She regrets to inform us that he is pronounced deceased, at 10:45pm, at the scene of a car accident on Highway 5. Identity confirmed by one JX. "Do you know JX?"

It is his good friend and driver of the car. They have been hit from behind, the car totaled.

That night I sleep in my dad's room, unable to go back to mine. I wake up sixteen. Age of autonomy. Shelter of my parents' bed. So old and so young at the same time.

DAY 3
Pieces of the Whole

1

Everyone talks about the weather that day. It was remarkable before the strike, clear blue and forgiving of any mood. Hard not to be in love with something, someone, anyone, really, in the wake of its romance, 8 a.m. and gorgeous already. But then a tower was on fire and people clotted the intersections. Suits and heels and cell phones, faces looking up. Is it a bird? It's a plane.

I once heard that if a hologram image shatters, each of the shards will hold the entire image it held before, not just pieces of the whole. Probably on the Titanic, sinking passengers noticed the qualities of the cold night. They saw their breaths freeze in the air and felt the dark sky press against their skin. White on velvety blue on gray. A spectacle of a night made more remarkable by its event. Ever notice how that works? In trauma, textures almost talk. Colors slide and sing. Voices stick and ring round and round in your memory, like a badge on the day. A time capsule, each thing discrete, definite.

On the Titanic, there were 1,500 stories of 1,500 passengers who never surfaced, and 700 more of those who did. And inside them, stories upon more stories that drowned or bubbled up to pop into the air, adding to the weight of the world. On 9/11 there were too many stories to hear. Too many to catch, capture, capsize. Three thousand died but millions watched. Like a hanging in the square, for all the world to see. Legacies stopped that day. Legacies began. Stories multiplied. How could you ever hear them all?

2

It's hard to tell when my story began. Was it the moments before the strike? When all I felt was the morning on my skin and the excitement of the first day of class? Or was it four years later, another time another town, hearing the diagnosis of Post-Traumatic Stress Disorder? Did it start before that? In the moments I couldn't find my reliably sunny disposition, and craved only to do violence to the jerk I worked with? Was it the panic attack and raw nerves triggered by construction noise outside my office? Or, did my story start years before that, when a coroner showed up to my house at midnight with a hole in her stocking and some very bad news?

So many stories, I thought I knew that were mine. But late on the night of 9/11, uptown and downstairs from the apartment where I was staying, I picked up a street-level pay phone to call home while monstrosities of machinery trundled down the avenue, pulled on trailers, chevrons of black vehicles, with sirens and red lights escorting them. Across the street a young man and a young woman stapled a piece of paper to a telephone pole. Receiver to my ear, plastic baggie of coins in my hand, I heard the operator say, "Calls are free in an emergency zone. Please place your call."

Emergency zone. My stupor cleared, fear finally seized me. I couldn't remember who I'd call, if anyone after all. Fear settled over my shoulders like a cloak I'd been shrugging off and I didn't know if I could cogently converse if I tried. After eluding disaster all day, it took the recording of a payphone operator to make me realize it. Cool, calm, no-the-fuck way. The night was blacker, clearer; the receiver heavy, sturdy, cold. I hung it up. I crossed the street. I looked at the lone piece of paper the couple stapled to the pole. Missing: Trey Smith, Age 22. Brown hair. Green eyes. Works at Cantor Fitzgerald. Please call . . .

By the end of the next day, fliers clogged every open space at eye level. Fences. Windows. The bases of statues in parks, bus shelters, telephone booths.

3

People call it shock. But in the moment, it feels soft, quiet, fuzzy and strangely clear at the same time. Time gets suspended. Not real time. Mind time. Time travel. When it's over, you open your eyes and days have passed, or moments. And all you did was open your eyes. I imagine awakening coma sleepers feel the same. Go to sleep very deeply one day, make your revolutions around your inner world, and then emerge with bedsores and achy bones you can't account for. No memories beyond the ones you took to sleep with you long ago.

Maybe I went to sleep long ago. I certainly didn't feel like it, living actively into my dream of moving to New York City, studying playwriting, becoming a bona fide writer with skills. I felt wide awake on 9/11, sunlight streaming through leaves as we stood in line to give blood. But I was tiptoeing on the surface of something. It was all unreal. It wasn't sinking in.

Now, I don't think it was possible to sink in: to meet the devastation we were witnessing with full awareness; to jump from one landmass of consciousness to another as the world as we knew it broke away from itself, into a new reality. To be fully aware of that in the moment the dust was rising and the crushed souls were flying away, would be to die inside immediately.

COLLECTIVE'S VOICE: Dave

The night before—no, wait—start sooner . . . .

A week prior. Yes, a week prior, I was on top of (Windows on) the world looking down on the vast city . . . in awe. Face pressed firmly against steel-cold glass, I mapped out the ride I'd take home to Brooklyn from 115 stories up.

The night before. On 9/10/01, I was in Tower 1, 15th floor. Later I spent a few minutes in the promenade looking up. Straight up. In awe of what stood before me, higher than the eye could see. Recalling a conversation of a friend who said his daughter had expressed fear over what would happen if the towers fell because Nana lived nearby. Nana told the little girl that if the towers fell, they'd fall in the other direction and Nana would be all right.

The next day they fell. Nana and thousands of others were not all right. Those who passed were fine, I believe. Those who remained were faced with picking up the decimated emotional towers of life now very different.

DAY 4
The Skill in Grief

I was listening to my boyfriend talk about coaching high school soccer. He was saying that the younger players with less technical skill play with more brute aggression than advanced players. "They want to plow through each other," he said, "because they don't know yet how to get to the goal another way."

For both kinds of athletes, the end goal is the same: to win. But without skills and strategies to deal with the other players on the field, and the ball in play, the game becomes about brute force. Who is more forceful than whom?

Brute emotional force

I laid this thought as a composite over grief. If you don't know how to handle it, but you have to get through it—because life tells you that you have to: your job expects you back on Monday, your relationships need you—then what effect does the brute force of mustering through have on you? And on your people? Now, in the near future, farther down the line?

Do we stuff it? Get aggressive with others? Channel the

aggression into work? Get addicted? Go shopping? Ignore our loved ones who know what we're like when we're grieving? Implode because it is too hard to handle? If we don't have resources, community, and skills to support us while in pain, what effect does grief and trauma have on our relationships at work and home? How does it affect our life trajectories? In getting to the bigger goals, past surviving—for those who can do any more than survive.

Bruised, but breathing

In 2007 I went back to New York on a research trip. Every person I interviewed who was in NYC on 9/11 spoke of their lives at that time, in some element, as having taken a nosedive in the years since. Deep depression, severe anxiety, change of career, change of plans, flirts with addiction, writer's block, dealing with loss and grief on other levels. Were we lacking skills to deal with what we saw on that day, and experienced in the weeks and years that followed? Internal eruptions and self-directed attacks matched the external meltdown we witnessed.

I spoke with a good friend who volunteers for hospice, sitting vigil with people who are dying. I asked her what led her to that life choice and she told me about a loss she experienced early in her life. She didn't know how to handle it, she said, but long walks saved her. And a friend who was willing to sit with her in her grief, just sit and listen and love her while she grieved, saved her.

What saves you?

We're deeply in now but there's more exposed than answered. In this exploration, I wonder how others have handled their pain. What saves you in deep grief? Do you cook? Take long walks? Craft? Chop wood? Run and run and run long distance? Work long hours? Sleep?

What skills have you gained in grief that will help you the next time around? Or that you can share with others who are also hurting? If you're deep in it now, and there's no skill in sight, what's your body's urge? Sometimes I would get an urge to pump my legs, like on a bike or leg-press machine. I just wanted to push and push and push. When I told a friend, he told me to do squats: stand, squat, repeat. I did. Right there in my kitchen. I cried. My body knew what it needed.

After a recent loss, I practiced yoga. I could hardly wait to get to the mat each day. By the time twenty-four hours had passed, my tensions were high; tightrope quivering; fear, sadness and anger roiling. I would bring it all to the mat, and for the time I was there, let my body and breathing take it over. Let it go. I also had a therapist who was yoga for the mind and emotional body, who offered me skills to reach perspective each time something new and painful surfaced.

Are you lost? Are you okay? What saves you?

DAY 5
Shared Grief

Dreamtime loss and opening

This grief project is entering my dreamtime.

I dream I am in the childhood home of Lydia, who lived down the street from me when I was growing up, until her family lost their house and lived in a van, four girls and a mom. The one time I saw their dad, he drank a beer in the front seat, gold foil glinting off the bottle neck, and then he was gone. Lydia and her sister moved in with us for a while till their mom found a way to bring them back together.

In the dream, I am adult. I find myself out of place in someone else's intimate space, like I have teleported here, acutely aware of myself. Her house is shot through with sunlight, empty and shining with polished wood. I feel we have to get out before the realtor and new families walk in on us. I am with someone very dear to me and we have to get out to find someplace to talk through this, a dreadful heaviness we are both feeling.

My dear companion is reticent to leave but he doesn't tell me that. Instead, he jokes, and when I drop my phone on the floor and break it, he kicks the pieces apart so it will take longer to pick them up. He doesn't realize the importance of getting out of this house. That it belongs to other people and they don't know we are here. That we are just borrowing it, I am only coming to get him. He keeps dragging his feet.

My anger flares. Impotent against what is bigger and out of my control, it melts at once into tears. He has lost his wife, his daughter in a nasty divorce. He cannot defend himself. He doesn't have the resources to handle the legal battle or the emotional one. His daughter is learning that he is a bad man when, in reality, he is hobbled by hopelessness. He is believing it, too. He can't see a way to fight for his worth, or his child.

I am crying. At first, he is not. When he begins, I feel bad for making him cry. For making him feel. But happy that I can help him by crying for him, sharing his loss. In my sleep, I can feel my body heaving. In my dream I ask him gently, "Why?" And in my dream mind I am hearing, "Why? Why? Why? Why?"

We cry together there in that sunlight. Then I wake up.

We were trapped in loss that started a long time ago. The only way out of the dream was crying together.

COLLECTIVE'S VOICE: Nicole

I've been through substantial loss this year ... though divorce is not really a death, perhaps a release .... It is fascinating and reassuring to see these swirling similarities. To breathe it in, really feel it ... whether it is yours or someone else's ... or both. That's some serious human connective tissue.

DAY 6
Emptied Empire

The streets of Manhattan were a ghost town last night. Empty. Looking for an open restaurant in this city of restaurants, Duane, Kate, and I were turned away by a concerned floor manager who wanted his staff to get home as soon as possible. The city was an empty movie lot. New York was gone from its own streets.

This morning, there were more people on the street but were we ever quiet. And walking slow. Having nowhere in particular to go, nowhere to be, turned the New York Minute into a funeral procession, hardly any singles on the street, most people with families and groups of two or more. People were close to each other and quiet. At the sidewalk café, there was implicit understanding when they didn't have chopped beef at noon, or home fries, or when we had to make way for the produce to be delivered at the same time as we ate. A sirened vehicle drove down 2nd Ave. and everyone quieted to turn and watch it pass.

Everyone was attentive to each other. We looked at each other. We listened. We nodded at people crying. Looked at each other as if we all had the same secret exposed and there was nothing to do but search each other's eyes for absolution.

After the café, I walked past, in daylight, the intersection where I had watched a young couple put up a "Missing person" flier the night before. Now, all four corners had light posts covered in fliers.

> "Missing Neighbor. Last Seen 9/11/01. Gregory _____. 26. Red Hair, green eyes."
>
> "Angel _____, 42, probably wearing a polo shirt and khakis, Hilfiger leather belt and shoes."
>
> "Katie _____. Curly brown hair. 29. Wearing the top in this picture when she left for work."

Details in death, in denial, in every last hope till we know for sure. There, finally, were some of my tears. I had wondered why they couldn't come.

Concentration is beyond me, though homework looms. Sense memory in acting class: smell this scent like you'll never smell it again.

The burnt smell, turned by the wind and sent up over Manhattan tonight will not be forgotten.

TVs on everywhere. People gather around them.

Nothing else matters, in shops, at work. We all understand each other's silence.

The nod. The gift of a greeting.

Yesterday, walking seventy blocks with the rest of lower Manhattan, stunned, quiet and walking. Walking.

DAY 7
Quiet Is Alive Here

Photo: Lisa Slavid 2014 ©

Waxy oak leaves clicking in wind
wheatgrass's sun-scraped stalks
buzzing things with wings
quiet is alive here

Different than a room left still
inhabiting absence

Here emptiness is full
full of humming, full of life
all in praise of stillness

As if the chaparral
shaking with wind
is snickering:

Even stillness isn't silence
Even death isn't death alone
All around, life clamors in

In sunlight, voices, heartbeats, time
to populate even grief,
to shape its pain,
and to save us from it.

DAY 8
This Is Really Hard

When David died, something happened to my face. It drained of expression. I couldn't be happy. I couldn't be sad. Stone set in. What would have happened had I shown some feeling?

Church was the worst. Music would play. History would float from the place I grew up on Sundays, calling back my brother, my grandfather who died three months before. Calling back time that was a whole lot different and a whole lot easier. Tears would threaten. They were pressed back at all costs. I didn't want to show anything. Because people would put their arms around me and tell me they understood, when they most certainly did not. I didn't understand. People would be achingly nice. They would watch me with sweet faces, from a distance.

High school was hard

I hated the way people looked at me. My life, I was David Teeter's sister. He was a year older, and super cute. In second grade the phenomenon of girls talking to me so they could get to know my brother began. After he died, I was still David

Teeter's sister. But to the people who didn't know him, I was that girl whose brother died.

Pity sucked

I hated what felt like pity when people would express their condolences. I didn't know how to accept it as anything else. I didn't know there was just sadness. Just condolence. I didn't know how to accept theirs without consoling them back, saying, "I got to grow up with him. I'm sorry for your loss, too." I said it because I didn't know where to place their generosity. I didn't know grace. There was only loss and hiding out from people whom I had yet to see since my brother's death, in case they hadn't yet heard the news. I would sweat bullets and dart around the nearest corner thinking I might have to tell them.

Writing this is difficult

I hate sending something out into the world and thinking, "I am being self-indulgent." I hate looking in on the Twittermall and thinking, "What am I offering here? I need to sell this harder." And saying back to myself, "There's nothing to sell." It's weird, this compulsion that something's worthy if it is trade. I offer this product. You offer that. When beneath distraction, protraction, transaction, there is this emotion to feel, this grief state to speak out, this experience to be and to release. I'm given to wonder, like I did in high school, "Who's looking?

What are they thinking? Is this bad? There's that girl who talks about death all the time."

Sharing is easier

My friend Tania said to me, "You carry grief for the rest of us. You actually feel it for us." But I don't know if I want to. I don't want to carry the water for the world, or even my community. We all have our jobs, I know. You clean houses, your neighbor drives the bus, your brother manages the bank. We pay each other for services. I carry grief for people. But that's not what I want to trade on a psychic level. My job is not the one you pay someone to do for you. It's the one you invite to help you bring the groceries in. Help you lift that heavy load. Help you to see that gorgeous light I see for you just ahead. See it? Just one more step.

This journey brings light to the system. The personal system. The communal system. Our bodies have to grieve. This is not an invitation to dwell in the dark, it is a voice calling us to connect, to find another side of this through each other, or nature, or art, or routine, through life outside us. There is another side.

I want to acknowledge that sometimes the dark is too dark, starts out dark, remains dark for generations, and it's barely even possible to be in the presence of so much loss, eruption, desertion. This is when I wonder if we can sit together in the dark, and eventually, together, take it step by step to a different place than we started. Till we make a thing, take a hand, accept an offer, place a call, listen for a voice inside, note a movement in our limbs toward a thing outside us that can help us, we can miss the path in a dense wood that will draw us deeper and hopefully through. We're not all going to see a path. But we have more resources together than apart, to find a way.

Emotion is hard

Have you ever noticed that in a relationship, when a couple is fighting, the one who is less overtly emotional seems to have the upper hand? The emotional one is flailing about trying to get the one who's not exhibiting emotion to feel something, anything at all. Meanwhile the one who is trying "too much" gets labeled over-emotional or sensitive.

I bet that would happen less if the individuals in the system shared the emotion that is there to be felt, together. Isn't it easier together? Easier for both? For all? Emotion, reaction, grief, they are entities. Trauma happens. Elephant enters room. What is the reaction? Any? I pray for everyone that every elephant that enters the room is gassy. Flatulent beyond repair. The elephant is an entity, to be seen, heard, supported, and guided back to the savanna.

Anger is hard

I have a pregnant friend who got angry because a guest brought their cold germs into her house and made her sick. Her pregnancy has been anything but a cakewalk, and now she was sick. She shared this anger with her small circle of friends and supporters, to a range of replies. "Don't be mad!" one scolded her. "You'll hurt the baby!" Others said things like, "Be positive, you can pull through, you're tough, if anyone can handle this, you can!"

She got a touch more miffed. "I'm expressing the anger so I CAN let go of it. It'll do my baby a lot more harm to keep it in and let it wreak havoc on all my other emotions." She got mad, let it go, and the fever and cold she picked up moved through her system in a couple of days, different than the weeks of sickness she had seen before and was afraid would return.

My writing had an angry hue the day I wrote this. I woke up surly. I worked in the yard to get it out of me, and when it remained, I thought, "Okay, what about anger in grief is there to write today?" And here it is. We are not angelic. We are not "nice" without consequence. We can't hide a part of something major in ourselves without eclipsing more, important aspects that help us be seen and loved and successful in the world.

Surfacing

Like it did each summer day before David died, the sun shined flat heat on our earthen driveway after he was gone. Celery grew, salty from the clay in the garden. The heat pushing through cotton, the sweat drying on skin of every summer day was a reminder that we had bodies, that he didn't.

One night, Steve came over, my eldest stepbrother. Steve had graduated to his own life years before. But one night here he was. Our family was under summer's pall. I wonder if he felt the lid over the top of us, because before anyone knew it he had walked into the front door, out the back door, and jumped into the pool with his clothes on.

Our pool was one of those above-ground beauties. Steve is a big, tall man. He lumbered up the wood stairs, splashed over the edges, lurched like a sopping hippopotamus, laughing at the crowd of us he had drawn to the backyard dusk, tempting us to feel something other than our gaping emptiness in the waning light.

That led at least two others of us to topple in, limbs submerged, underwater sound, which led others to grab towels, pull up patio chairs. Screaming and laughing at the saving grace of absurdity, we were released like atoms.

Hard is not the point

While writing this, a noisy, yappy, yelpy chorus of coyotes rises nearby. The whole community of them bounces their voices off the hillsides, sound swelling in their barks and howls, a choir, one organism, the pack of them.

There is something to feel here in the depths of us. Something to touch. Something to share. And something to howl together if it is too much to howl alone. The illusion of grief is that it feels so deeply, sadly alone. Everyone grieves, from the moment of separation from our mothers' wombs.

This darkness spares no one. But neither does the light, shining alongside it like a prize.

COLLECTIVE'S VOICE: Susan

I discovered a quote from Winston Churchill after my husband died that helped me: "If you're going through hell, keep going." There IS another side here . . . . On the day that Bruce died, two friends came and just sat with me. They didn't do anything, they didn't say much. They did bring me a milkshake, since I thought that was the only thing I might eat that wouldn't come back up. I never understood until then the tradition of just sitting with The Widow, and I will be forever grateful to them. Their presence helped, helped keep me grounded, and I knew I wasn't alone.

DAY 9
Something Is Happening Here

Something is *happening*. A groundswell of feeling. There are tears and light and thanks, and pain healing itself. All flowing like a river. There are conversations and openings. There is awareness borne of talking. Understandings created right in the middle of conversation, like cells are multiplying and dividing in our very words.

Reset

A few years after the 9/11 attacks, I lived in LA. I was tired. My learned resources were failing me. My scrappiness was wearing me thin. I thought this sense of loss and isolation and feeling out of control of my life was the beginning of the way it would be for the rest of time. I thought I was losing my mind.

I moved north to a tiny beach town where I had close friends from college days, and hit reset. In Santa Barbara, I was still looking for my mind. But I was starting ground floor: First take care of home. Then food. Then work. Then future. One thing at a time. I didn't know this wilted version of myself, but I continued.

Down by the river

One day, I sat at my receptionist's desk, looking out on the parking lot, questioning what I was doing but knowing it would get me to the next thing, and the next. It was like breathing, each day was. First in. Now out. Doesn't matter if you don't understand how you got here, breathe in.

I set down the phone and, out the window, saw a river of butterflies, floating by. A current of Monarch butterflies was streaming—gushing—through the parking lot. Thousands upon thousands of butterflies, black and orange and fragile enough to look lighter than wind, but clearly muscling through it midway on their 2,500-mile journey from Mexico to Northern California.

I watched the migration till it dwindled, about 20 minutes after it began. It felt like a cleansing. And a prayer. Down at the river. I think that's what they call a baptism.

COLLECTIVE'S VOICE: Christyna

Something is definitely happening here. I feel connected, seen. I empathize with and honor this human experience with its embarrassment of rich details and the universality of the themes beneath.

August is my month of mourning. Last year was the third year of this tradition, and August lasted from mid-July through September. It was a surprise, a weight, an illness of its own.

This year is different. I am not alone. Though I am tempted to isolate, this year I know this to be a temptation, not unlike the cheap candy in the foyer at Halloween. This series . . . , the spaciousness of the invitation—it calls me to the higher resonance of grief. I am awed and humbled at the meaning/emptiness of the human experience. I am face to face with the exquisiteness of life, whole.

DAY 10
The Sound of Silence

August 2001

My first week in NYC.

Concrete towers.

Cars—rivers of them.

People—tireless, endless, forever grids of hundreds of people in view.

I walk by a homeless kid sitting against a building. Taxis honk by, it's like the City Symphony Orchestra. The kid's cardboard sign says he's deaf. Past me flow conversations and arguments and footsteps, all a piece of the sound. I imagine what it's like to not-hear this city, bombarded as I am by this place so new to me, overloading every sense. I turn off the sound, let the quiet inside dampen everything. I imagine a city under water, life moving about all the same, silent.

September 2001

New York City was quiet for three days after the strike. Not a taxi blew its horn. Sirens the only sound on the street besides car doors closing, self-aware voices subdued.

October 11, 2001

I'm headed to class. People cram into the train. A few minutes into the ride, I see the conductor look at his watch. The train slows, stops. He says, "I got 8:46." On the intercom, he announces a minute of silence. We are a steel tube stuffed with humans. We make no sound. A minute passes. The train picks up motion again, then speed. The silence remains.

August 20, 2011

Today, I think of the ritual of "sitting with The Widow" that a reader, Susan, shared on Day 8 of this project. I'm thinking of memories and conversations that have surfaced since Day 1. Some recollections feel like blunt trauma themselves. I'm listening, like I do every day, for the memory that wants to be told next. And I'm hearing silence. Silence. And more silence. Silence that follows death, comes close behind trauma, sinks into the crevices and takes hold, to cocoon us for a while in safety between what once was and what will be.

DAY 11
Patterns in Chaos

Sometimes when the silence starts
it doesn't stop for a while

It becomes a density rather than a sound

Words are buried deep

When that happens

like today—

it's hard to communicate outward

But if I go out in nature
patterns in chaos
communicate back

They organize the silence
till the speech comes back

DAY 12
Another Country

There's something womb-like about Santa Barbara. When the sun hits the ocean, it bounces a pinky-yellow haze between the mountain faces and the islands off the coast. It's amniotic. Hypnotic. The stillness here is a balm. I have returned more than once to restore. I am here now, to make space for this writing journey.

Today I sifted through memories and kept feeling one I didn't think directly related to my project. But I promised myself I would listen to intuition and write the story that wants to be told each day. Whenever I stall, fear, doubt, I hear my best friend's voice in my head. She dares me sometimes, in the most loving of ways, saying, "If you don't trust you, trust me."

So I wrote the story.

Resurfacing

As I began to introduce it, I remembered that I left Santa Barbara under some very sad circumstances. And that while this town is my restorative retreat, I understand a healing needs to take place here while I am exploring grief.

I used to live here. I used to love here. The two memories
that follow, written after a loss in December 2007, bring that
sadness to the surface—to meet, feel, acknowledge, and then
continue on the journey.

"The Car"

PEMA: We're here to—. Do you have a—? What were we telling them?

RUDY: That we, uh, that . . . .

KHAN is listening intently in the huddle we created, waiting for
one of us to finish a sentence.

RUDY: Our friend and colleague parked his car here before
Christmas and then died in a plane crash and we're here to pick
up his car.

KHAN blanches.

KHAN: I'm, my gosh, I'm—.

We are blocks away from LAX at a parking garage. In Khan's
eyes, you can see him calculating, trying to recall news briefs,
flipping through imaginary etiquette books, while we all stand
in this circle in the parking garage wondering what to do next.

At the counter, I pull out the death certificate from my
notebook. I pull out my ID.

The longer I wait for the people to find the key—to type in the date Michael parked, to find the car in the lot, to call each other on the intercom and disappear and reappear and give me more forms to fill out—the more closed-in my vision gets. My breath is shallower by the moment and my fuse is short. I see only a wall of keys on the valet board behind the counter. The surprising lashes of the young woman helping me. The piercing in the side of her lip, like a metallic beauty mark. The people on either side of her looking forlorn and unsure of what to say or do. I am stoic against the tears that want to come, in waves.

I get the keys. Valets have pulled the car out front. Rudy and I hug. We cry. I get in.

How do I start it? The radio comes on with the car and plays a commercial of a new show Michael's business, the one we work for, invested in. I get out and tell Rudy the synchronicity. I go back to the Mini, and I can't figure out how to adjust the seat or see the odometer or open the windows. My brain is too fogged from the black interior, the tears on the reverse slide down the back of my throat, the impossibility of focus on these simplest of mechanics to get me out of this garage.

I am finally out, I pull into the sunlight. And immediately I drive to the side of the road. The tears are heavy and my breath is jagged. Fucker. Jerk. Dammit. This is *not* my drive. This is his view and his scent. The performance hum under my ass and my feet is *his* ride, his familiarity.

The wheel under my hands is glossy wood and a paper-smooth leather. Its contours cradle my grip. There is life here all around me and under me. I am breathing it and applying myself to it, moving with it.

I drive fast. Fast in his fast little car. Change the radio when I hear music he wouldn't like. Dance wildly in the driver's seat. Absorb the man in his absence.

Another country

I sat on the Mission steps tonight. Conquerors always get the best real estate. Just before sunset. Cloud cap over the sky. Distant ocean. White plaster and red tile roofs of homes in the foreground, and the main thoroughfare moving with cars. A few tourists.

I watched the cars head toward home in the twilight. And in them imagined people of another country. I am the tourist. In their land. Watching their way of life, imagining their different language thoughts as they plan dinner, mull over the day, look forward to seeing their kids. Habits I know but at present am set abroad from.

I go home to cook dinner for myself for the first time since before Christmas. Conversations outside of work are still hard to focus on; language goes all watery before they're through. Grief is another country.

DAY 13
Adventure and Anger

The confrontation

After Michael died, I tucked away the program from his memorial service. It had four pages of full color pictures of him. Every time it showed up, in a file or a pile or a book I had slipped it into, I would tuck it again.

One day last year, it turned up in a pile I was organizing. "I have to stop," I told myself. I held the program. Looked at Michael. It had been nearly three years. I liked to remember him alive. His spirit was so vibrant that it seemed . . . out of place to dwell on the memory of his death.

"Where am I going to put this?" I muttered to myself, looking around. I always ended up tucking it away because I could never think of a spot that would protect me from getting sad or awkward when I saw it.

This time, I had recently read a Feng Shui book. Everything has a place, it said. And the two thousand dollars that came my way twenty minutes after I had swept and reorganized the money corner of my studio did not go unnoticed. "I'll put Michael in the 'helpful people' corner," I decided. I pinned the program to a wall in my bathroom. It had to go somewhere. If I spent time thinking about it, the program would get tucked again.

Call to adventure

Two mornings later the phone rings. It's Kate. I'm not up yet. She apologizes for calling so early. But she has something to ask me. "Our company is sending someone on the Lilith Tour to report from the road and I think you'd be great. Can you go on tour for the summer with Sarah McLachlan and a bunch of girl bands?"

I have spent late winter and early spring building a website and new identity for my business. I am two days away from launching. A lifetime nomad, I think, "Maybe this is one of those times when people say 'No' to an opportunity because it just doesn't fit." And so I say, "What I wouldn't have given ten years ago to do that. I know some twenty-four-year-olds who would be perfect for this job."

But before I hang up I say, "Listen, this is a wild opportunity. Just so that I feel good about my decision, let me call you tonight and tell you my answer." She agrees. I hang up the phone. I get out of bed. Go into the bathroom. And what's the first thing I see when I turn on the light? Michael's picture. And what's the first thing I hear in my head on seeing it?

"Always go."

It was Michael's motto. Got an opportunity to go some-place? "Always go." Got a venture that sounds wacky but holds water? "Always go." Someone offering to fly you to Patagonia to trek the moonscapes of other planets? (Have you seen pic-tures of Patagonia?) "Always go."

I hold my breath. I'm going on a concert tour.

Road love

Several times on the road—with eight adults sharing a narrow travel coach that drove all night to get to the next concert city, sometimes fourteen hours away, in which we would build up, host, and tear down the concert village in one day—things got challenging. Like, new-challenging, crucible-challenging, mys-terious-there-is-no-answer-to-this-oddity challenging. But on the whole, it was beautiful, magical and often mystical.

We eight fell in love. Stars in the eyes, birds tweeting around our heads, fell in love with each other. On days off, we'd arrive at our hotels, part ways, and twenty minutes later be calling each other to see where we were spending the day.

A week in, I observed that our bus captain looked, and even felt, familiar. After talking to him one-on-one, I realized he looked so much like my brother, David that if my grand-mother saw him, she would cry. Weirder, Josh was sweet, he was generous, he was sort of our advocate and protector, and he was a really big dork. All of David's dominant attributes.

And there was Leslie, who shared my birthday and, coincidentally, was born a year and a day after we lost David. As it was, there was a gorgeous generosity in our group. Each of us had space to learn from each other, space to allow each other's mistakes and missteps, space to laugh our asses off inside those mistakes, and space to grow into this beautiful human experience that surprised us all.

Grit-your-teeth mad

Fast forward. It's about ten days till the end of the tour. The morning before my birthday. And I'm angry. Gael, my work partner and bus mate has pissed me off. As we leave our hotel, boarding the bus for a long drive back to the US from Toronto for the next day's show, I can't shake it. We have practice, Gael and I. He has told me more than once on this trip that his girlfriends tell him he makes them crazy. And I get it. I use the practice and tell him why he has made me mad. He apologizes. I am appeased. It's over in five minutes. The bus takes off. And I am still livid.

What is up with this anger? I am simmering in myself, I am so mad I can hardly sit still, let alone talk to anybody. Everyone is peppy with the energy of having had four days off, excited for our next city. What is wrong with me?

Howling-raving-aching mad

Then it hits me. It's the anniversary of David's death. Today. "But why the anger?" These years later (it has been twenty-three), if it affects me, I usually feel sadness. Anger still simmering, I think of Antoine's innocent, even joyful, generosity when he listened to me tell him I was mad at him. I try to sort out the genesis of this feeling. And, like an egg breaking over my head, I get it. It occurs to me I have never been angry at my brother. Out of twenty years of grief and three recent years of what felt like whole healing, I had never thought to be angry at him for dying and leaving me behind.

Adelia was the first person I told David had died, when she came to pick us up for summer school class. I remember thinking I had never seen tears pop into someone's eyes instantly like that before. One second she was driving, the next, we were stopped in the road, tears spilling down her cheeks.

Sitting on the bus, teetering at the precipice of the raging source, I feel anger sweep over my body like a tidal wave. Tears spring to my eyes, like they had in Adelia's. My skeleton melts inside my skin. I can feel my muscles are going to give out on me. I climb into my little berth, close the curtain to make the black, womb-like space that rocks us to sleep each night, and sob. Grief and anger wrap my body into a coil, as I sob and sob into my pillow. As I scream at him—into my pillow. I cry angry, searing-hot tears. And fall to sleep.

Golden

When I drew the curtain hours later, we were in creeping border traffic over Niagara Falls. I slipped out of my berth, puffy-faced and spent, carrying this body density and this spirit clarity. In a moment, Abbey joined me in the back lounge. She didn't say anything but her face was kind. And then Jenn joined us. We sat together looking quietly out the window. And then Shanna. Light reflected off the water we were crossing, its volume grand in sound and size. It was beautiful, vast, legendary. Trucks carrying produce drove next to us and cars slipped forward and back in the slow roll.

Golden hour light slanted through the windows and caught our skin. Cameras came out for pictures. Conversation came in spurts. Then laughter, then antics. All subdued and sweet. I came to life again. Berthed, rebirthed, crossing a border named The Rainbow Bridge, reentering my country, buoyed by golden light and motion and love.

COLLECTIVE'S VOICE: C.S.

My loss goes back to Dec 31st, 11:00 a.m., 2001, when my husband died almost instantly of massive heart attack. Our three children were five months, 9 years, 12 years. I have always felt the loss of being his partner in our lives that we built together. Raising my family without him is very lonely. I've often felt the twinge of loss when I realize that he is missing one more milestone in our children's lives. I would feel sad for him that he is missing it because he loved being a dad so very much. Only today, after reading [this] passage, did it click in me that I feel left behind.

Today: My second husband left for his annual two-week trek to Burning Man. I feel left behind. It just occurred to me why I feel so sad today—it triggered the feeling of being left behind. It makes more sense to me now how I feel today. I feel a little bit less burdened in realizing this connection.

DAY 14
Value

I was 18. I was wearing a periwinkle jersey T-shirt dress with a buttoned breast pocket. I couldn't get my white, pilled, pedestrian, hand-me-down bra strap to not show. I kept looking over my shoulder and pushing it under the dress.

Meanwhile, I was testifying against my mother in arbitration. It's what disputing parties do when they want legal resolution without going to court. My family was at war over who would get what money from the insurance settlement from my brother David's death.

Outside in the waiting room were two families that used to be one, pretending as if the other wasn't there. There was my grandfather, who looked like David, with his kind eyes and gentle deflection, holding a young child on his lap, and my grandmother looking and sounding as she had each time I'd seen her, like Lucille Ball, red lips, red hair swept up, constant motion engaging others, playing the ditzy jester. This time she was chirping her attention anywhere but toward me. Inside, the arbitrator explained to me that to calculate the division of the settlement he would need to compile the monetary value my brother added to the family, in terms of housework, outside chores, "anything you can think of that delineates his value alive." The arbitrator also needed to estimate the monetary value of David's love for our mother, who sat there at the conference table as I answered her lawyer's questions with the haughty attitude of a teenager forced to do something against her will, pushing my bra strap compulsively under my dress.

Cache

I have been thinking about value. And currency. And debt ceilings.

Say you're saving money for retirement and the system goes bust. Money is not enough to sustain you. What can you live on besides money?

I watched my grandmother age. She sat alone in her apartment, where friends and neighbors circulated, yes, but she lived solo for twenty years after her husband died. Our conversations on the phone were twenty-five percent current events, twenty-five percent planning the future and fifty percent memories. She had a store of them. Each day she would take a trip in her mind. Today, Glacier National Park with the grandkids. Tomorrow, Niagara Falls with the Wilsons after our honeymoon. Next week, leaving the office inside a moment's notice when Orin got called to the War, setting up temporary housing with milk crates and the other war wives who had taken the train to Seattle from San Diego for basic training. They were scraping together every last minute of six weeks with their men, before service to country took them and turned them into the men they would become. Or wouldn't.

What if currency were not something to sock away, or something to horde, not printed on paper or debited in digital? What if it were something to embody? Exercise, build up, share, employ? Today, tomorrow, on rainy days, retired days.

What are your currencies?

What do you value?

Who are you for people?

What if money fails?

What do you trade for the good of yourself, your family, community?

DAY 15
Phenomena

Will

The night David died, there was a thirty-minute window during which I was wide awake and praying with every last muscle of my will that he come home. It had sounded like things were fine. But the more minutes that passed, the more logic smothered fine.

As a girl, I had a will that could shut everything else out. I would set my belief on something, and it was only a matter of time till the situation materialized. In that thirty minutes of waiting—for normalcy or devastation—I prayed like a stadium of believers chanting to change the tides of the moon.

"Let him be okay he's going to be okay make him be okay." There was no space between pleas. I was a freight train. Fear propelled me. But the more I prayed, the more I gained strength, hope. Until—whooosh! The sensation in my body, and in my mind, was as if someone threw the generator switch to OFF. Silence. Nothing but silence. I didn't breathe. I didn't think. And from somewhere in that silence I heard or felt or knew the words, "He will come home or he won't. What is done is done."

The coroner showed up instead of my brother.

Impact

I hadn't seen JP since the night David died. They had been friends since third grade. They were getting ready to go out. He was wearing a new acid-washed denim jacket, and showing it off.

On this night, JP came in without the jacket, and said they'd had to cut it off at the hospital. He told us what he saw that night, this 17-year-old witness to his best friend's death. He came to our house by himself, let himself be surrounded by our family, and told us what he had seen.

The three boys had walked to the Jeep. David hopped in the back seat. And JP said, "What are you doin', man?"

David said back to him, "Get in." He'd been in a bad mood that night so I wasn't surprised to hear it. But I was surprised to hear JP say that they'd had a system. A habit. A hierarchy? JP in the back seat. David shotgun. JX drives. On this night, David jumped into the back seat without impetus. Later, a car driving ninety miles per hour plowed into the back of them and threw the back seat from the car, killing David on impact with the road.

The Jeep was totaled. Its roll cage was shoved fully forward.

JP and JX escaped with bruises, and an internal loss I can only imagine to this day.

Witness

They had been driving on the freeway, miles and miles from our neighborhood, several suburbs west of our high school. JP told us that even though it had been late at night, eyewitnesses had pulled over and run to the scene. They turned out to be a kid from one of my classes and his family.

Headway

How do you communicate "bereft"?

Some losses take away the lost and cancel out everything else. For me, language darkened. I don't remember talking a lot after David died. Expression lived somewhere as deep as my heels, or in some internal universe from which I had no transportation. My words were gone. Everything was quiet in me, like the silence that fell when the generator was switched to OFF.

When I heard JP's stories of that night, when I heard that the eyewitnesses were people we knew, and about the coincidence that saved JP's life and took David's, I stubbed my toe against something that I could hold onto. A rock I could pick up off of this blinding path, and turn over and over in my hands, my existence. The coincidences were the only recognizable elements in the whole of this unrecognizable scene. It was like being in a black night and seeing two stars. Illumination, barely. But enough to consider that maybe I wasn't in this darkness without a map, somewhere, and a plan, eventually, that I would understand, sometime, step after step after step. But first, silence.

DAY 16
Interview: New York City, 2007, Part 1

P: I have a memory of you guys visiting New York or New Jersey and being stuck here.

B: Right.

P: And I have a memory of you saying—were you guys supposed to be on one of those planes?

B: Flight 93. We were supposed to fly out on Monday night, the tenth, and there was a fire at Newark Airport—major fire in the luggage area, so they had to cancel flights and delay flights. We waited around for a while that night but we decided, "You know, forget it, we'll just get on the flight in the morning, and we'll go back to my sister's house."

So the United person said, "I have a flight in the morning and a flight at 1:00 in the afternoon."

I said, "Let's take the morning flight."

So she said, "Okay," and she put us on that.

And Tom, just as we were about to walk away, he said, "You know, by the time we get back to your sister's house, get to sleep, and then it's an early flight—we're basically going to get a few hours' sleep and come right back. What's the rush? Why don't you call work and say you're not going to be in at all tomorrow?" (I was trying to get back so I could work a half day.)

So we turned back to the counter person and said, "Actually can we take the one o'clock?"

And so, the next morning . . . . To wake up and see that.

P: Did you connect it right away when you saw it?

B: No, because when we first woke up, the first plane had hit the World Trade Center. But that was one of the Boston flights. So they hadn't . . . . Flight 93 hadn't crashed yet in Pennsylvania. So, just the shock and horror of seeing what happened. Then we pieced it together, and we didn't remember the flight numbers, but when they said it was from Newark to San Francisco—

P: When did you realize that? You heard it on the news?

B: Yeah.

P: What did you do? What happened in your gut or your head, or with each other when you heard that?

B: You know, I think it was, you wanna say relief but it wasn't relief because it was still such horror at what happened. I don't know, I feel like so many people felt so close to all of the tragic events. If that were another situation where I was flying to Colorado or something and I missed the flight and took another one, I might feel more personally singled out, or "Wow, that was a near miss." In this case it was so overshadowed by . . . just the tragedy all around. It almost felt selfish to think, "Oh thank God."

Plus, it was personally overshadowed by the fact that my sister's husband worked in the World Trade Center and we hadn't heard from him. She couldn't get in touch with him. So, she's freaking out.

P: Yes.

B: We did have a sense because the [time] that he left that morning was a little bit late. She was thinking he might not have arrived to the World Trade Center, and that if he had, he would not go in. But still, the fact that she couldn't reach him on his cell phone, she was flipping out.

P: When did you guys finally hear from him?

B: Three o'clock.

P: Holy—Wow.

B: Yeah.

P: Were you guys all together until that time?

B: Yeah, so, you know, it was just one of those—everybody in Westfield, the town, lost fifteen people. Most of them were men. The whole town, neighbors, you could hear people wailing. And everybody who didn't have somebody who might have been in the World Trade Center was galvanizing around the people who hadn't heard.

The fact that we narrowly missed that flight, like I said—it's only in retrospect, to realize that I wouldn't be here today. On that day, it didn't really register.

P: Has 9/11—whether that day, that coincidence, the experience with your family—how has it registered over time? Between then and now, have you related to it differently? How do you carry the memories of it?

B: You remember what it was like here. The world stopped. There was not a soul walking around that wasn't stunned. We were all zombies here, emotional. You're just, hugging strangers. This . . . you can't describe [it]. And then we got on the plane [after a week of grounded flights], we went to San Francisco, and when the plane landed everybody applauded, because people were so afraid to fly at that point.

I still was in the bubble of being consumed by what happened. I got back to San Francisco, and it was distant. People were definitely—I think most people in the country took that day off, even a couple of days. At [my company] they gave everybody off the next day. But a week later, which was by the time we were able to get a flight back, it was business as usual. I heard the most trivial conversations on the street, like, "Oh that's a cute skirt!" And I'm thinking, "How can you say it's a cute skirt? How can anybody even think about a skirt?" I felt like shaking people, "Don't you realize what happened?" But you know, it was across the country.

You remember being here. It was so real here.

P: Yes.

B: The smoke, you could see it, you could smell it, you could almost feel it in the air.

P: I understand there were so many other, bigger things going on than you taking that plane.

B: Right.

P: But then retrospectively, thinking that it's not only a plane that you skipped like any other plane, it's one of the planes that changed our nation forever and, in addition to that, one of the planes that had all this communication from it . . .

B: Yeah, to think of the terror of that, yeah—

P: . . . calling family and friends.

B: I thought about that. I thought, knowing Tom, he would have been one of the guys to stand up and help.

P: How do you begin to wrap your head around that? Once you move past the experience of being with your family, your brother-in-law coming home, taking in that trauma and the media every single day of what has happened, six years later thinking, "One of those seats was mine."

B: Maybe I haven't processed it. Every time I tell the story and people are, you know . . . . Their jaws drop. I almost feel like I'm telling someone else's story. So I have this distance with it. But maybe it's me not dealing with it, or . . . I don't know I just have extreme faith in the universe. Who knows? Ten years from now, or whenever . . . my number's up? So I can't quite feel lucky—I do, not to sound ungrateful. I do feel lucky. But those people didn't deserve it. I'm not going to celebrate and think I'm special.

DAY 17
Interview: New York City, 2007, Part 2

In 2007, I returned to New York City during the week of September 11 and interviewed several friends, and one stranger, who had been there during the attacks. Reading the interviews and in listening to the conversations now, I am struck by the depth of processing that took place as we talked. Six years after the fact, we were still in the deep, working it out. I encountered emotional treatises on government action or inaction, and long reports on how people were seeking, personally, to understand ourselves and our places in a post–9/11 New York, country, world, and existence. Fear, sadness, guilt, patriotism, shame were all in heavy rotation. For me, the interviews are a snapshot in time, each voice testing the tide, as we pulled our way through a roiling current. Here my conversation with B. continues.

Conversations on fear

P: I interviewed my teacher from that day. She said, "I was immediately sad because I knew we were going to go to war." She said, "From that point on, I have felt sad because the way that we felt on that day—how terrified we were and how we had no idea what to expect next—that's the way our country, our government is making Baghdad feel. That's how Baghdad feels every single day, still after all this time." She said, "To be there, to live there in New York City, and to experience that happen and then to know that we are by extension part of—."

B: Repeatedly.

P: "—other people's experience of that terror, I just can hardly—"

B: And, historically, inflicting that terror and more. Hiroshima . . . .

I went to a seminar three or four months ago. It was about being fearless. Al Gore was the speaker and he was phenomenal. He talked about how we had an opportunity at 9/11 to respond. Imagine if we had responded peacefully, with love and understanding, instead of going into this military "eye for an eye." Where does that get you? Violence begets violence and the cycle continues. But if we had responded in a way that—you know, the *whole world* was with us. You remember seeing candlelight vigils in Germany and Japan—our previous enemies! The Soviet Union. Here's the world coming together. And we have since, I mean if you think about the perception of the United States in the world right now, it's never been worse.

P: And what an opportunity to shift the direction of our entire way of doing things.

B: This was the subject of the conference. If you live your life and your actions are based on fear, even if you think you're taking strong actions, if they're the result of fear—like in our nation's security, we've got Homeland Security and our mission in Iraq is for security of the United States, and our way of life and democracy—it's all still based in fear. It's acting for the wrong reason. It's acting on the worst instincts of human nature . . . .

And how presumptuous of us. And how desensitized everybody is. Every day in the paper? Every day in Baghdad? . . . Some bomb. Some explosion, and it doesn't even register anymore. The current administration fosters fear. Every time they've done something wrong, they raise the threat a level. To distract people to "Remember the fear! Remember the fear!" . . . . We've turned that word "terror" into "safety."

P: You were at the center of the terror that this "safety" is in reaction to. Does that affect how you think about it?

B: I think it has to do with your relationship with and your idea of death. For Tom, he's very afraid of his death, and mostly of death of people he loves. I don't know, maybe I've put up a barrier but I'm pretty stoic about it. If I was on that flight it would have been my time to die.

P: It goes back to that theme of fear, becoming fearless . . . .

B: If you're afraid of death all the time then basically death's got the better of you. Because you're living your life with that end in mind, and you're not really living your life. It's like Elizabeth Edwards. I loved what she said when she'd just found out that she had recurring breast cancer and there was no treatment for her. People were stunned that she was continuing with the campaign. She said something like, "You know, I really have two choices. I can start to die or I can continue to live. I want to continue to live. If I quit the campaign, then I'm starting to die. I'm not gonna do that."

I just thought that pretty much sums it up for all of us. You can start to die or you can continue to live. And that's courage.

DAY 18
Spiders, Delinquents & Hate: Life Is as Big as It Is Small

Spiders

It's not that I'm deathly afraid of spiders. I don't love them. We are not friends. But I am friendly. I give them wide berth. I evacuate them in a flying Tupperware out the door, and pick up the empty Tupperware in the morning.

This altercation was different. I stood on a chair aiming a spray bottle of kitchen cleaner, the strongest stuff I could find under the sink. I held my breath, fought back chills upon chills over my body, and unleashed streams of the stuff on the black widow perched under the shelf. My plates were going to go there. But here was this hefty black spider with a red hourglass on her belly. That's like the radiation symbol equivalent for arachnids. This one, pretty as she was, couldn't live. If she stayed in the house, she could come find us in our sleep and kill us. If I threw her outside in a Tupperware, her escape could come back to haunt us, or the dog who spent most of his time in the back yard.

It lasted too long. I sprayed her and she ran into a crack in the corner. I flooded the corner with spray and she came out briefly to struggle with the spray till she crept into the crack again.

It was awful. I get chills writing about it now. I talked to her between fitful outbursts, apologizing. I told her to make it easy on me. That one of us had to die here and it wasn't going to be me, and I was sorry it was set up this way. As I talked to her, and pleaded for her quick death, the effort got longer and longer, kitchen cleaner dripping down my arm, my jaw tight from clenching. The truth was, she wouldn't come find me in my sleep. If I got near enough to her territory, she would defend it, like any of us would defend ourselves and what is meaningful to us. But she had the power to harm me. And this scared me sufficiently to end her life.

Delinquents

I never went to jail. I never got caught in cars with boys. When I started bringing home girls, my conservative family's teeth clenched. But beyond—or maybe to tiptoe around—my queer-leaning sexuality, I was well behaved to a dysfunction. If did things right, I got approval. If crossed a line, I was a bad daughter/sibling/community member/child of God. Approval was more appealing to me than being a bad anything. Thus, my outward-appearing halo.

At twenty-two, I went to live with my mom for the summer. We hadn't spent that kind of time together since I was a toddler. Story is she left then. By the time I was, oh, I don't know, a teenager, I could count on my hands the times that I had seen her.

At twenty-two, I was adult enough to write my own story with my mother, not the family story. She was funny and pretty and charming. She was loving and welcomed me to her part of the US. I planned for six months. We faxed letters back and forth, and I asked her all the questions I would ask a prospective roommate . . . what are your preferences, when do you go to sleep, do you like having guests over? I wanted it to be easy. There was a lot of time and a lot of legacy to run under the bridge.

Fast forward.

It's our first weekend together. And I discover: I am still more child than adult. I am in a strange land with no spending money. The house is empty of food. And my mom seems to think nothing of flaking on the time we'd been planning all week, to instead go to the movies with some guy that walked in the door fifteen minutes ago.

She's at a movie—one that I'd been talking about for days because I saw it before I arrived. I'm pacing in the apartment. I'm thinking, "Twenty years apart has come to this?" I'm thinking, "What the hell?" I'm stringing four-letter words into new alphabets. My mind is fireworks, my body is fireworks, because somewhere in my girl brain, as adult as I had entered this experiment, I am abandoned, I am not worthy, I am a puffed-up pride-bomb bursting with: *Do I really not matter?*

I didn't know what to do with my anger and confusion. I looked at the sliding glass door, open to the balcony. Plumeria scent drifted in on soft air. It was sunset. It was summer. It was too beautiful to be so far from home and so alone. I looked at the furniture in the room: an elliptical machine, a TV, a love seat, couch pillows, dresser drawers. I growled. I stomped my feet. I seriously considered throwing every piece I could lift off the balcony. I imagined clothes flying, wood splitting as it hit the ground three floors below, the glorious sound of glass exploding as the TV followed. In my imagination I felt liberated from this rage as I watched the elliptical machine fly over the balcony wall.

I had never imagined destruction like that before. I had never felt the associated release, the get-back-at-you, look-at-me, I-really-really-need-you acting out that goes with neglect. For the first time I understood how young people could get into so much trouble. Could steal cars and wreck things and drug out to numb out.

I left the room quickly. I locked the door behind me. I sought refuge in the apartment building's empty laundry room, tiny and loud with washers and dryers, and screamed.

Hate

I come home from a weekend away and find my old pickup truck has been vandalized. The headlamps and mirrors are busted, the windshield is shattered, the wipers are mangled, the antenna broken. My stylized rainbow bumper sticker is slashed and hanging half off. The small, square "Equality" sticker is equally slashed. And scrawled in big black letters across the tailgate are the words, "Never cunt dyke." There's a smiley face drawn on the door.

The cop that comes to take the report refuses to record it as a hate crime.

It is three weeks later. I'm sitting on the bus. My truck has been set on fire. Destroyed by flames outside my house, underneath some low hanging trees and in a neighborhood of tinderbox, Victorian-era houses. The city firehouse is around the corner. The inspector is investigating my friends and exes, embarrassing them where they work.

When the inspector questions me, he pulls out the community newspaper. On the cover is pictured my vandalized car and, inside, my angry quote, complaining that it wasn't recorded as a hate crime, despite the obvious indicators. He holds it up, sneers, and tempers an angry voice while saying, "I see you don't think much of the force that is trying to help you here."

I'm on the bus. A loop of the four weeks prior plays in

my head. I look at the people around me, following the law, minding convention, dressing appropriately, being protected by their civil rights and recognitions. I want nothing than more to chop off my hair, dye it bright pink, pierce my face. I want to break laws I am not protected by. I want to do unspeakable things to convention, till it's raw. Toss the rules that betray you when you're not part of the game.

DAY 19
My 9/11: Where Were You?
Part 1

I have stopped in the telling of this story several times now. I have erased, rewritten, changed tense. My story is no more profound than anyone else's that day. Less so if we're keeping score on the level of tragedy. It baffles me, how difficult it is to remain focused on the words when trying to type. It's medicine and I don't want to swallow it. I've told you in detail stories about my brother's death, my family's emotional ridges, my view of the way it was for others. But, for the love of things holy, if I can't stand where I was standing and tell you what there is to tell.

I'm here

The sky. Unbelievable and blue. New York. Oh my god, I'm HERE. The morning, I can feel its coolness in my nose when I breathe. It lines my lungs. I round the corner heading to class and two guys from school are running past me to the corner. I hear them say, "Building on fire . . ." as they pass. Six minutes, it's all we have till class starts. They've drilled it into us for a week: don't be late! And I think, "I wonder what they do in New York City when there's a building on fire." I'm from the suburbs. We have room for fire. I slip down to the corner and see what I see. It's the World Trade Center, those twin towers down at the end of the avenues. I have only just learned they are the way to tell south from north in the jungle of concrete I encounter every time I emerge from the subway. People are converging on the corners of the intersection. It's a Superman movie. I think we're all looking for Superman. The sun is so bright, it looks like studio lighting.

Fire

The hole. There are flames all around it. It is way too high for any fire hose spray to hit. How will they handle that here? They can't extinguish that, can they? My heart begins to sink but I haven't noticed yet. I have begun to count instead. How many floors, estimating, has the plane blown into the building? How far do the flames reach into the building? How many offices and how many people at work at this hour? I realize my minutes are up if I'm going to be on time to class. With a last thirty seconds, I imprint all of this as a picture into my memory, so I can finish counting while I sit in class. I don't know why I'm counting—it's an urgency I am meeting in the moment—till I enter the room, find a chair, hear the end of the calculations in my head, and realize what they added up: the estimated number of dead to whose houses the coroner will be dispatched tonight. I begin to cry.

We sit in a circle in a huge studio with a linoleum floor.

God, this story continues.

Reflection

Thirteen of us sit in chairs, sandwiched by floor-to-ceiling windows lining the immense fourth floor. Our teacher introduces herself. She goes with it as much as theatre training allows: use the moment. We don't know what is happening outside other than there's a hole in the World Trade Center tower. We can hear phones ringing beyond the walls, hear sirens screaming endlessly down the avenue, and feel tension in the air around us getting so thin it will break. A couple more people are silently wiping tears from their cheeks. I look past the shoulder of a classmate. Out the window facing the building across the courtyard, I see the reflection of smoke, billowing impossibly thick up the face. A row of students lines the windows. I watch them, riveted, not moving, watching. At one point, we hear screams outside and the row of people—all of them but one person—ducks their head and dashes from the window. I wonder what made them do that.

Globe

Class is over. An hour and fifteen minutes has never lasted this long. We go downstairs and the courtyard between our school buildings is full of students and teachers. Everyone is gathering here till we receive more instruction. Two planes. Two buildings. One collapsed. Pentagon. Pennsylvania. Military jets ordered to shoot down planes still in the air. Carl, a student who has come to the university from a career in the military, is ticking through the events that occurred while we sat in class. As he does, we get word that the other tower is collapsing. I sink to the concrete step. I see people all around me but don't register faces. "They've done it," I think. I don't know where the thought comes from or who "they" are, but I am proud that I think I know something important, as if that will help me. I wonder what to do with this body in this city in this morning when "they've done it." What now? Feels like a we're a scene in a snow globe: fixed, shaken, waiting for the snow.

Blood

I walk out sliding glass doors from the lobby. The tiles inside are deep brown, the light coming in the door and that to which I emerge is otherworldly. It is so bright, the light. People are walking toward the avenues. Where am I going? No answer. What am I doing? No answer. I follow my feet to the right. Toward the avenues.

A woman stands in the middle of the street, wearing a backpack, holding a "GIVE BLOOD" sign, black letters on a piece of white paper, printed by an office printer. I wonder how she got that done so quickly? And now she's directing people to action in the street. She is haloed in sunlight. You can see it lining her hair, her backpack, her arms. She is pointing people toward the hospital two blocks west across the avenue. I haven't been to that side of the Village yet. The avenue runs like a river between where I go to school in the East Village and the West Village on the other side. Looking across, I'm not ready for unfamiliar territory. But my feet keep moving. My body needs a destination.

I cross over and join a line two blocks long. It doesn't move. We stand a long time. Other people come along and hand out bananas and water and some sandwiches and food items and say, "You'll need to eat. Take one and pass them down." I put a banana in my backpack. We hear again and again, after the line hasn't moved, that there are virtually no wounded in the emergency room. That the give-blood lines are all winding around the city. But there is no one to give blood to. I wonder what I am doing there alone. I leave the line and walk back toward the direction of school to see if I can find anyone I know.

DAY 20
My 9/11: Where Were You?
Part 2

Oh my God

After I leave the give-blood line, the rest of the day is a series of memories out of order. Walk across 6th Ave. Back to the school. They are clearing out the lobby to accommodate triage for the nearby hospital. Someone leads a handful of students to administration to use the landline. Cell phones are out of order. The cell towers were on top of the World Trade Center buildings. I call Suzy. People crowd the office, waiting to use the phone after me.

"I'm okay," I say.

It's early in California. She's groggy. "What? Why?"

"Suzy, turn on the news."

Her partner turns on the TV. "Oh my God."

"I need you to call my family."

I give her my brother's number because he can reach the rest of the family. I give Suzy my grandma's number because I want her to hear from Suzy directly that I am okay.

Dust

I walk south. I don't know why or how far. The school's back door is at 6th Avenue and 11th Street. (When they shut down Lower Manhattan the next day, they close off 12th Street and below.) Shadows of leaves dapple the sidewalk and the people on it. We are stringy. That is, no one really focuses on anything and we are not walking anywhere in particular. I see someone on the steps of a church. I wonder if that is the place to be right now, I wonder if I should go in. I decide there is too much going on outside in the world to go away from it. I don't know what I should be doing, but I know I want to be available to it all. I don't know what is going on and I want to. In a city of strangers I run into Bill, someone I met at Mia's place on the Upper East Side. It's where I'm staying till I find a place to live. He tells me he had to get out of Tribeca. It's the area of town closest to the rubble, the smoke, the epicenter. People walk past us going north, covered in dust. We are standing in the way of foot traffic. He tells me he'll probably see me tonight at Mia's. He needs someplace to sleep.

Futile

I am back in the vicinity of school. I see Rael and Rob and Cici, and maybe a few others. We are aimless, walking, unsure, but begin to look for another place to give blood. Over our shoulders we watch the smoke gush into the sky. We wonder if we should be breathing the air. We realize there's nowhere to go to get away from it. The sun is hot now and we have been walking for a while. We reach a hospital in the East Village. We can contribute. The line is not huge. There is a woman sitting at a small table in front of the sliding doors, and next to her, an immense standing banner lists who is not eligible to donate blood. Two people in our party of five make that list for being gay men. We swirl on our own planet of discombobulation and disbelief for a moment, our long walking mission futile, and move on.

Fall

CiCi and I walk toward Uptown. We walk thirty blocks, forty blocks. Around fifty, we get on a bus. It moves more slowly than we walked, traffic barely inching northward, cars feeding into the avenue from every street. People pressing up the avenue in droves. I understand the meaning of droves. Once in a while, I see one person walking south, in contrast to the bodies moving northward. Invariably the person is crying, hand on face wiping tears, shoulders pressing forward. The bus is so packed we hardly breathe. Tensions are high. We get off the bus two blocks later having rested long enough to push out and walk another twenty. On the way we talk about class. Theatre. Stage. Experience. The play this might turn into someday, characters walking, walking, walking their way through. How CiCi said she wished she'd never seen the buildings fall. How I thought that if I'd seen them fall, I might believe it.

COLLECTIVE'S VOICE: M

I watched the towers fall on NBC. I had spent a lot of time in that building on the top floor in Windows on the World restaurant and knew people who worked there. I wondered what became of them. My office at the time was five blocks north of the towers. Was anyone there?

We walked through the dazed and empty streets south to donate blood at Columbia Hospital—what else were we going to do? We were turned away, along with hundreds of others as well. It was there on 114th and Amsterdam that I saw the first people who were covered in ash.

DAY 21
Clowns, Cocktails, Suspension

Campfire

I don't remember arriving home that evening. I do remember passing bars crowded with people in suits, windows open and doors, cocktails, beers, wondering aloud, faces wide, heads shaking, news glowing like a campfire. Where else to go?

Vigil

The next day nobody knows whether or not to go to school. Late morning, someone posts its closure on the website. Our school is inside the Lower Manhattan cutoff. We stay away for the week. I find an apartment in Jersey City. During the week, missing persons flyers paper NYC. Union Square itself becomes a shrine, candles and vigils, posters and chalk, visitors paying respects to the lost, to their shock, to their city, through the night. I find myself walking there when I have nowhere else to go, leaning into the low park wall, feeling the cool spatter of rain. Watching, listening, waiting for an answer in the presence of all these people. A channel change. A tide.

Here now

When class resumes, we return to the circle, questioning the substance of an art degree in the wake of our city's event. The loose, watery practice of actors and writers pretending to be something we're not. What are we doing here? Our teacher summons the fires of fury, future and past, imploring us to understand that the voices of artists are the voices our culture needs most, as it finds its way through this breakdown. That imagination is not pretense, that creativity is deepest truth.

Fuel

I can't go to Ground Zero or get close. I just can't. One night, I share a seat on the PATH train to Jersey with a man whose boots and jeans are covered in thick dust. It is the end of the day. While everyone is tired and quiet, his body seems held up by only his skeleton, the rest of him slumped into the seat, swaying. No one speaks.

The smell of jet fuel and demolition wafts through the train car.

Possessed

One day in a mask workshop, the teacher tells forty of us, sitting on the floor in a circle facing outward, to each put on the smallest mask, the clown nose. We learn the proper ritual for putting on a mask. You let it hover in front of your face, breathe into it as you set it to rest, and it comes to life. Your body becomes the mask's. It's a possession. In a crowd of people in masks you forget there are people you know underneath them. They screech and howl and strut. They laugh and stutter. And barely do you notice the person delivering the character.

On clown day, the teacher counts to three and has us all turn at once to face into the circle. We are quiet. There is Nico and Rina and Rich. In red clown noses. Dev and Calvin and Maria and Cori and Christina, a room full of people in a circle sitting on the floor, sunlight settling in late afternoon corners. No one speaks.

I lose it.

Crack

I start to giggle. I mean, a room full of people, in silence, with straight faces, and clown noses. Everyone's clown face swings to look at me, and I in mine am laughing. I can't stop laughing. My voice gets high, people smile, tears come to my eyes. I double over. When I sit up everyone is still looking at me—and

I laugh harder, double over again, and as I am bent, a sob catches in my throat. I press it back, confused.

Quieted, I take a breath, look up, see the red noses, all their faces quietly watching me, some straight, some with surprise, and lose it into guffaws. Again, I double over. Stop. Catch breath. Let the fear of maniacal sobbing quell the outburst.

When it is over, I feel alone. I feel the swell in my throat, my heart, my chest, like I am going to crack, and I wish I could let myself. Break in the moment. Be taken by clowns.

DAY 22
Return

Day one

I'm in New York:

> I used to live here.
>
> 9/11/01 was my second day of grad school.
>
> I watched flames and smoke from a street corner near class.
>
> Many students left soon after.
>
> I didn't have an apartment yet.
>
> But I stayed, realizing that I had prepared for this day so thoroughly that I sent one set of storage boxes to my parents in the Midwest and the other to Suzy in California: In case I died, I didn't want my parents to have to wrap their heads around the evidence of a life lived creatively.
>
> Being here was a dream.
>
> There was no better place for me to be in the world.
>
> Where would I go?
>
> Eventually, the grad-school-in-NYC part of my life ended.
>
> I've been back lots of times.
>
> But I'm nervous now.

Because it's the first time since I lived here that I've allowed myself to feel the trauma of the events.

I'm a late bloomer.

And I had an iron cage around a tiny heart.

Since nearly losing it—and by losing it I mean white-knuckling my mental health, pilfering food and living on the charity of friends and strangers—I started a slow return.

This visit is part of it.

Not worth my tit

The overarching theme in my 9/11 interviews:

New Yorkers see the crushing need for peace more than anyone else I've talked to.

War is reiterating, on foreign soil, the death, destruction, fear, and anguish that knocked the wind out of our nation on that day.

The more life we extinguish, the less ground we gain. The less distance we travel in healing our grief and the schisms of the world.

> NYC graffiti:
> "Our grief is not a cry for war."
> "We were born innosent and kind." [sic]
> "One Love. People get ready."
> Your Tat is not worth my Tit.

"here is new york"

The previous quotes are from photos at the New York Historical Society photographic exhibit, "here is new york: remembering 9/11."

The photos are presented simply, no frames, 11" x 17" prints hanging on string with binder clips, filling all the wall space and strung overhead across the rooms as well. The exhibit covers the space of two large galleries with photographs taken by scores of photographers at or in relation to 9/11.

They show survivors, World Trade Center rubble, layers of dust, writing in the dust on windows of abandoned cars, emergency workers, onlookers, blast views, planes headed into the towers, jumpers, distressed onlookers, stunned, dust-covered survivors holding their foreheads in one hand and a water bottle in the other, hand over the mouth (the international sign for grief and disbelief), missing flyers, impromptu memorials of candles and flowers and cardboard, butcher paper in colored markers, chalk on the sidewalk overflowing with sentiments, shopkeepers and volunteers feeding emergency crews, prayer stations, revenge signs reading "Wanted Dead or Alive" with a picture of Bin Laden, a Humvee squeezed onto an antique, tiny downtown street, more dust, papers scattered about a church graveyard, countless tears, that clear clear 9/11 sky, NYC concrete corridors, every last person facing the direction of the smoke, watching in disbelief, subway stop memorials, people staying together, strangers in each other's arms, firemen holding hands on their way into the pile, kids' drawings, missing sisters and fathers and migrant workers and traders, blood, twisted metal, mettle, post-apocalyptic organization, blue sky . . . .

A habit of lists

From my desk here in Santa Barbara, composing from materials I've collected in my return trips to New York, my research and interviews and story sketches, I thought for a moment that I might not post the quotes I copied from the New York Historical Society exhibit photos, worrying that I might be bombarding people with 9/11. But it strikes me over and over that what I'm doing is healing. And others, from what I heard in response to my original stories, are healing along with me by watching, listening to, or otherwise being a part of mine.

The quotes:

"Not in our name."

"This is no time for cowboys." (Sign around the neck of a life-sized John Wayne cut-out.)

"The news makes me cry."

"Patriotism scares me."

"END WAR" (Written in block letters inside a ONE-WAY sign.)

"PWPD/FD Meet Here—FLFD" (Written in the ash and dust on a van window.)

I also compiled a list of names from some of the photos of missing persons flyers, to press their letters into paper, feel the grooves their names made on the back side of the page. Later, after the fliers captured in the photos had been rained away, other people compiled more lists of names, along with a few phrases about each person, to serve as a public memory. I imagine the list makers felt compelled the way I was, to collect and compose a body of loss, to make real and mourn each individual absence, to keen into the volume of our collective mourning.

As I write, it's raining here on the California Central Coast. Land of the Maxfield Parrish sunlight and clouds, views and mountains, sky. It rained in NYC on 9/11, the day I was visiting the Historical Society exhibit. I find it interesting that out of two galleries of walls filled with photos, the one that struck me the most was a simple cityscape, point of view looking down an empty avenue, even more distinguishing, the absolute clarity of sunlight caught in the photo. I got stuck in this photo all those years ago, and that's where I've been walking around since.

Going back to NYC in 2007 was the first time I faced what I'd been eluding. I went to the observances. Let my grief surface. Let myself be someone who grieves over this trauma. Before I returned, I was so interested in how it is we move on from grief, how it transforms us. But being at the World Trade Center site as the names were being read—as the rain was falling, as, across the water, lights shone in remembrance, upward into a black sky—made me realize there is no hurry. Grief takes its slow steady time, unwinding like the coils of a snake languishing in sunlight, loathe to leave the rock that has been warming it. Grief transforms. We are changed in it. But first grief is grief. Its own spirit and will and breath. Before it moves through, it inhabits. The exquisite journey is to cohabitate.

DAY 23
Chat at the End of the World

[Nico]   Woman.

[Pemsi] Yo.

[Nico]   Whats up?!

[Pemsi] A little nighttime.
         You?

[Nico]   Mid-life.

[Pemsi] Still?
         :-)

[Nico]   Still.

[Pemsi] Oy, my friend.

[Nico]   Seems like every time I turn around, I'm just in the
         middle of it.

[Pemsi] Zen, man.
         That's very Zen.

[Nico]   I try.

[Pemsi]   What are you in the middle of?

[Nico]   Crisis.

[Pemsi]   This is poetic so far.

[Nico]   I'm sure it'll get more so.

[Pemsi]   Here's some pop-psych on the fly: the middle of
          "crisis" spells "is."
          You . . . is. You're BEING.
          . . . Om
          —okay, I don't want to run amok with your problems.
          Are you ok?

[Nico]   I suppose so. I started dreaming about plane crashes.
          I feel like screaming constantly. I thought of buying
          cocaine. I want to move to Vermont. I have been
          spending more money than I have. I haven't been
          writing. I eat cookies and drink scotch. None of it
          seems to help.

[Pemsi]   Ugh ugh ugh.
          I don't know what to write first.
          Me. I have been seeking some kind of therapy—
          psycho-, group, medical, or metaphysical—for at
          least the past year.

[Nico]　And?

　　　　No luck?

[Pemsi]　Tons of luck actually

　　　　I have PTSD—Post Traumatic Stress Disorder

[Nico]　From?

[Pemsi]　Well. Watching the towers on fire.

　　　　And a few things leading up to that.

　　　　I pretty much thought it was a crock.

　　　　But I guess it wasn't after all . . .

[Nico]　Have you watched *United 93*?

[Pemsi]　. . . because all this therapy type stuff has been

　　　　leading me out of my . . . anxiety, burning head, full

　　　　body breakout of itchy red spots, antisocial behavior

　　　　and mean-spiritedness, extra weight . . .

　　　　. . . let's see what else, the feeling of not being where I

　　　　think I should be, feeling like two to twelve different

　　　　people, and general malaise and malfunction.

　　　　I have watched it, yes.

[Nico]　I hated it.

[Pemsi]　Did you see the movie and it's giving you dreams?

[Nico]   Yes.

         I think it was criminal.

         It is great. It is a perfect film.

         But so were Leni Reifhenstahls films.

         Excuse the spelling.

         I wish I hadn't seen it.

[Pemsi] Why did you see it?

[Nico]   I was told to.

         I'm sorry to hear about the PTSD.

[Pemsi] It was the best thing I had heard in three years.

         I was like, "PTSD! Thank god, I knew something
         had tweaked."

[Nico]   My nightmares have been different since then.

[Pemsi] Since 9/11?

[Nico]   Yes.

         But you know what about *United 93*?

         It was a lie.

         The movie was a lie

         A crime

         If you ask me.

         I mean that actually. An actual crime.

[Pemsi] Seems to me it was a dramatic mimeograph of the newspapers.

[Nico] No—it is much bigger than that.
It is the definition of a hate crime.

[Pemsi] ?

[Nico] If I am allowed to make racist, one-sided generalizations of an entire people through any medium, that does not seek to raise understanding but rather raise fear, hate, anger, sadness, and otherwise further pain and suffering in the world, then I am committing a crime of hate.

[Nico] If, through my actions as a media-maker, I create a one-sided imbalance which seeks to shame, humiliate, and otherwise threaten a specific group, that is a hate crime.

[Nico] Filming *U93* and distributing it to thousands of theaters scrawls a message of hate for Muslims across our whole society, and does not once, even a little, seek to help us understand what happened, and why those passengers might be considered heroes any more than those who died on the AA flights that hit the towers.

[Nico] I ask myself why. What possible impact does this
film have?

It is war propaganda.

It is the voice of the empire.

It is the blind repetition of the official story. 9/11
TRUTH!!!

[Pemsi] My friend Gary said it kills off 3,000 people while
stroking heartstrings.

[Nico] And we pay $10 to slurp toxic stew.

[Pemsi] I saw a picture that looked like the nuclear sunrise
dream this week. Remember that one?

[Nico] Really? The dream?

Well what are we gonna do?

[Pemsi] Spike the soup.

Wake the shit UP.

My nuclear holocaust dream had me walking with a
camera down an empty NYC street.

There I am in the dream, the future certainly mortal,
and I have a camera that will get destroyed in the blast.

[Nico] Well, the one thing that's sure is that you and me'll
disappear.

[Pemsi] But I'm taking photos anyway.

[Nico]   That's wonderful.
         And very sad.

[Pemsi] That dream finally means something, Nico.
         If we're meeting the end, how can I possibly help, or
         possibly write fast enough to matter?

[Nico]   I sorta think you can't.
         At least that's how I feel about myself.

[Pemsi] But life is about doing, and if I don't do . . . then . . .
         Then what?? What is it all for?

[Nico]   Maybe unfair to project, but . . . I don't know. We
         live in a system that is complicated beyond what we
         can possibly process.

[Pemsi] I think you'll be annoyed with me for the book I'm
         writing.

[Nico]   What is the one thing, in your life, that if it had
         been different, would make the most change for you,
         right now?

[Pemsi] Nico, you have to breathe or something.

[Nico]   I breathe plenty.
         I'd never be annoyed at you for writing a book.
         What is the book you're writing?

[Pemsi] You know all the healing I referred to?

[Nico] But you're right, I have to breathe or something.
        What that something is I don't know.

[Nico] Do you ever do drugs?

[Pemsi] It's universal.
        And it's got ghosts in it, so to speak.
        But they're ghosts we know.

[Nico] Universal healing . . .
        That is wonderful—how do you give it to others?
        And who are the ghosts?

[Pemsi] I don't like how drugs make me lose control.
        I'm so airy already, I can't think on them.

[Nico] Ha!
        You are not airy.
        Do you think of yourself as airy?

[Pemsi] I'm from So Cal. :-)
        I believe anything is possible and I leave room for it
        in my life.

[Nico] Nah. I mean, I'm sure that's where you're from, but
        I've met airy.
        I don't think you are airy.

I think you are . . .
In tune. And sensitive.
That's not a bad thing.

[Pemsi]   Okay, that's better than airy, yes. But that being in
tune leads my attention away from the present . . .
like being able to remember where I parked.

[Nico]   Who the fuck really cares where you parked!
I don't know—I think you gotta keep it where it is.
I think you have something to say.
You're asking me what's the point, and all that?
I think you're much closer to having the answer to
that question than I am.

[Pemsi]   All that being in tune led me to a psychic, who
corroborated what someone else said, that I have
"souls stuck in my field."
So, I stutter, s-s-sou–field? Wha?
And she says, you have souls in your field from the day
you stood on the corner watching the towers burn.
And they are speaking.

[Nico]   REALLY?!

[Pemsi]   Then she channeled them.

[Nico]   That's fucking insane.

[Pemsi] So, for the past year, I have been writing this book. Because the stuff she said was profound and bone rattling.

[Nico] It rattles my bones
Just hearing about it.

[Pemsi] And your head and your whole belief system if you're willing to go there
My skepticism in tow, I have channeled a couple of them myself.

[Nico] And what happens?

[Pemsi] In the narrative or when they come through?

[Nico] Either.
Both.

[Pemsi] One time, I was craving peanut butter on a sesame bagel . . . ha ha there's more (but wouldn't it be funny if there weren't?).
I don't eat wheat. I'm allergic. I don't crave it. But I couldn't get the thing off my mind.
My breakfast didn't deter the craving.
. . . I used to eat bagels and peanut butter every day in NYC, before class.

[Nico] Crazy.

[Pemsi] So I kept thinking of them on this day, and even
         after breakfast, couldn't focus on my work.
         Said screw it, went to the deli, ate it. Tried to work.
         Couldn't.
         Finally . . . I was like, what? What?? Then I realized.
         It's not me.
         I got a pad of paper out and started asking questions,
         and the answers came out fast.

[Nico]   Someone else.

[Pemsi] Named Andy.

[Nico]   We are prisms splitting the light of our life.
         That's crazy, Pemsi.

[Pemsi] Yeah.
         An image of a firefighter, and a little kid three or four
         years old, standing at his feet.
         I talked to the psychic after that, and mentioned it to
         her, and she tumbled out with the rest of it, little kid
         and all.
         . . . and speaking of prisms of light, I channeled
         another one named Nancy.
         Her message was much longer and so amazing. And
         she spoke of the family of light.

[Nico]   Requiem aeternam. Et lux perpetua luceat eis." (May
         they rest in peace and may perpetual light shine on
         them.)

[Pemsi] You asked how you give universal healing to others . . .
         from what I can tell, you heal yourself, and then you
         share it, or better, you heal publicly so that people
         can heal with you.

[Nico]   Pemsi, though, you aren't responsible for channeling
         these spirits—you don't think you are do you?
         Please—that is such a crazy burden!
         What are you going to do with that?

[Pemsi] I don't know that I feel a burden so much as a
         possibility.
         It's been a healing journey, so I only get tweaked
         about the responsibility stuff when I imagine the
         world is going to end.

[Nico]   You are one of the few good souls. That's what I think.

[Pemsi] I guess what I mean is, I do feel the burden some-
         times, but I've always felt it . . . I just didn't know
         what it was till now.
         We have to just do. Whatever the thing is that we're
         called to do, whether the world is tipping its hat
         or not.

And I can't deny the presence of those hanging
around me, strange as it seems.
Strange is the new normal.

[Nico]   Strange is the new normal.
It is indeed.
Oh my god—my head is tired.
I need to drink some more and download some porn
and get ready for work tomorrow.

[Pemsi]   Yes, me too. All of it.

[Nico]   It has been wonderful chatting with you
And . . . Well . . . And hearing that you are healing things.
That is worth a lot.
I sorta wish we could toast or something.

[Pemsi]   Thanks, Nico. It's like a non-nuclear sunrise to chat
with you, all while still being . . . the bomb.
A digital text toast will have to suffice.

[Nico]   Digital toast it is.
Night.
Thanks for the good talk.

[Pemsi]   Night. Thank you too. [rainbow icon]

[Nico]   Ah!!!! You know what rainbows are, right!?!
Or are you taunting me.

[Pemsi]   Hope.

          Promise.

          Gay pride?

[Nico]   Oooooh—read your email—I think it might be at
          the bottom of the forwarded message. If not—I will
          tell you tomorrow.

[Bottom of forwarded message]

"Every time you see a rainbow, think upon this: I do set my
bow in the cloud and it shall be for a token of a covenant
between me and the earth. And it shall come to pass, when I
bring a cloud over the earth, that the bow shall be seen in the
cloud. And I will remember my covenant, which is between me
and you and every living creature of all flesh: and the waters
shall no more become a flood to destroy all flesh."

*Printed (with slight corrections made) from a 2006 Instant Mes-
sage chat with my friend Nico, classmate from grad school in NYC,
cohort in the school year that followed 9/11/2001. Bible verse is
Genesis 9:13, King James Version.*

DAY 24
Embodied: A Search for Healing

Julie Daley—a beloved coach, teacher, writer, healer, and wise woman—writes about and works with the feminine principle. Julie has worked with grief in her life and others'. She has taught classes to 9/11 widows in their transitions after loss, writes about the earth and our connection to it as humans, as women, and she explores female existence and spirituality, unearthing sacred awareness with each article and blog post.

I wanted to ask Julie about her work with grief, specifically regarding her closeness to the healing process of the personal and collective tragedies of 9/11. And we did get to talk about that. But where our conversation turned surprised me. Julie's listening, and her answers to my exploration, made way for a big share from me, and made me understand the deeper reason for our call, indeed for my whole thirty-one-day *Memory to Light* project: To witness, to be witnessed. The sacred call of seeing and being seen.

What follows is the big share and the wisdom in its wake. This is one small part of our rich exchange.

The story

Pema: In the last few days when I've been thinking about our upcoming conversation, it's occurred to me to ask about phenomena: if you've listened to people talk about phenomena that they experienced, if you ever talked about letting themselves be guided by supernatural phenomena, mystical phenomena, these very images and elements we've been talking about. I'm going to put a period on that and stop asking you questions and tell you something, because it sounds like all of my questions are leading to this anyway.

I had a really wild awakening about four or five years after 9/11. I had moved back to California a year afterward. It took me a couple of years to realize I had PTSD, and that my life, much like many of my friends' on that day, had taken a nose dive in certain areas. I left school because somewhere in the dark recesses of my mind, I thought I was going to lose my mind, and I'd better be in a safe place when that happens. And so I went back to California. I still followed an opportunity to study, but I left school proper.

Then, it did. Everything began to unravel. It kept regressing, and so I went further back, to Santa Barbara . . . a womb and a healing place for me.

Surprises

While I was there and living in the good graces of my friends'
charity and this community that I left a long time ago, I
started looking for what would heal me. All over my skin, I
had psoriasis that took over my body . . . . I was having panic
attacks. Everything about myself that I had known was gone,
or eclipsed.

And in my search for healing, I went to a massage therapist, a
holistic massage therapist, and she said, "By the way, you should
probably see if you have souls stuck in your field from that day."

I thought that she was a quack. But a few months later, I
couldn't forget about that.

So, I ended up talking to a psychic. I said, "Look, you might
be a good person to ask this, because it keeps coming up. What
do you know about, like, souls in your field or something?"
And she immediately started channeling. She said, "You have
thirty souls stuck in your field from that day, and this is what
they're saying."

Called

I was, of course, floored. At the same time, I felt this intense
release in my body. For two days that followed, I felt this light
coming through my head and out my feet. And I felt this clarity and this pure joy that I hadn't ever known before. And I
thought, "What do I do with that? What the hell was that?"

And so this journey that I started on August 11, has very much been about, "What do we do with grief? And why is it so hard to take on?" As I've taken these steps in these last days, I've realized, "We're all on so many levels of experiencing our grief, who am I talking to? Who wants to hear this? Whose mind am I trying to change?"

You know, you just said, "I have clients who say, 'I'm afraid to feel my body.'" One of the things that was channeled was this anger. [They said:] "Wake up. Wake UP. If only we had bodies to walk around on this earth and to hate our jobs and to make choices. If only we had our bodies. Wake UP."

Stored in our hearts

I am compelled to tell you that because I'm asking you to share so much. And because we're having these conversations about how *do* you know, how *does* your body know? How *do* you feel?

And you know, I have talked about this experience, but I have talked about it in kind of guarded circles, because those are people who died. People in our nation's consciousness, in their families' consciousness. Real people who had real lives and real loved ones and here I am saying, "Well I had this experience, with these souls."

I'm still working out what to do with that but suffice to say I have been compelled enough by the messages to follow another journey. And I'm noticing that this exploration of grief

I'm taking keeps leading to that, to what you just said, that this information is stored in our bodies and our hearts.

There is this whole question of waking up. I keep talking about waking up to grief enough to know that it will take you to the other side of yourself. It'll take you on a transformative journey.

Driven

Julie: Yes *and*. It will do those things, *and*, it is *not* linear. You have no idea what else is going to come. Where it is going to come from.

That is important to pay attention to because, as you were saying that, it was like something driving you—I don't know if it's you driving you or something driving you—to do this. As you started to tell that story, your whole voice changed. There was a lot of energy there. A lot of power there, about that story.

When I shared what clients say, "I don't know how to feel my body. My body feels like concrete." This dissociation from the body, that's the split between the sacred and the earth, the spirit and earth. And one of the things I know Llewellyn Vaughan-Lee [from Working with Oneness], talks about and that I've experienced in my own vision is that women have something here to share. It has to be shared for us to move forward as a species to heal.

Sacred body

It's so important for spirituality to come down-into, for us to bring our awakening and our awake-ness and our awareness down-into the cells of our bodies, because life on earth is a sacred experience. It's an amazing, beautiful experience and we're walking around like lollipops trying to prove it all. It's this glorious experience, which sometimes it's not glorious in the way we think of glorious, but it's all beautiful because we are feeling it.

When I try to tell people how beautiful it was when [my late husband] Gary died—I was awake, finally. I mean, I felt in every cell of my body, even though it wasn't what people would call a pleasant feeling. I was no longer sleepwalking. I was feeling. And that in itself is I think a miracle, that we are even here feeling in these bodies. That we're alive. It feels like there's something in those messages that you got about that.

Witness

Pema: There is. I've been spending the last six or seven or eight years trying to understand . . . who I am in relation to those stories, or who I am to speak for these people? The minute I say that, I realize I'm not speaking for anyone, I'm just sharing the experience. I'm telling the story. And as I build my identity as a storyteller, as I discover how much I relate to story in the world, as I say this right now, I think, "Oh, well look at that,

that's a safe place to be." If I am a witness then I can just tell the story as a witness rather than claiming this really far afield experience . . . .

Julie: Yeah, and it's interesting when you asked me how I worked with [the 9/11 widows.] . . . . It feels sort of parallel to what you're saying about these souls, because . . . the healing and all the stuff that happened is sacred. I can talk about *my* experience of being in the room but I can't share what—I have to notice the line where I would be disrespecting that sacredness. That's what I notice, I think, that you are articulating around these souls.

Pema: Right! Right. They are not mine to claim.

Julie: No.

Pema: They are not a soapbox to stand on.

Julie: They're not.

Pema: And at the same time, there are these messages that are coming through.

I had to go on this journey of understanding, of gathering up myself . . . wiping off all of the stuff that's not mine that I've collected over the years, and then pulling back up . . . what is mine? What do I want to do? What feels sound to me? And then in understanding who I am, is there a way for me to be a voice or a channel for that which has come to me, that is not mine as a claim, but is an experience, a life experience to relate that is universal?

Julie: Well, yes. Yeah, absolutely, because it's coming through you. That's what's happening. And trusting that if it's coming through you, it's all going to be revealed . . . .

It's like trusting yourself, trusting your heart, trusting your body, trusting that you can move through it, trusting in the sacred and the greater, whatever you want to call it. That it is holding you. When I was [on retreat] in Hawaii, I kept hearing these words: "So much is given. You are so loved. So much is given. You are so loved."

When you really get that, we are so held.

Pema: And when we're held that's when we heal.

Julie: Absolutely, whether we're held by a human being in somebody's arms, by a community, by ourselves, we can do the healing work, absolutely. That's beautiful.

DAY 25
Eclipse

Photo: iStock/Bowie Chan

Definition of "umbra": "The blackest part of a shadow from which all light is cut off."

The wind is high. The night is cool. The full moon is fully eclipsed, dark and disappeared in its umbral shadow.

But, curiously, the shadow never stops moving, and soon the skinniest of slivers begins to show the moon's light again. This time, it was fifty-one minutes of darkness. Umbrage. If we can just feel the quickness of that passage, or the continuity of it, perhaps we can remember, without seeing, that even the dark speeds toward the light. Even the dark is defeated soon.

From my project files, February 20, 2008.

DAY 26
Wonder

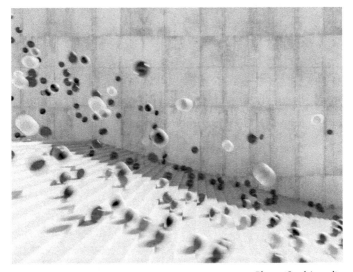

Flights. Of fancy.
Falling. Without fear.
Attacks. Of joy.

Can I take you on a visual and auditory catharsis?
There's an ad made by Sony for their BRAVIA TV. On
a perfect, sunshine day, set to the ethereal acoustic of

Jóse Gonzáles's "Heartbeats," hundreds of thousands
of rainbow-colored bouncy balls lace into a city view,
bouncing down a San Francisco hill street, in shot after
slow-motion-shot of color burst clouds.

Fleeing. In release.
Corridors. Of color.

I can't explain my tears as I watch it over and over. My
chest is light and my sadness is not heavy; it is turning
around and embracing me. I feel embraced by my sadness as if it is grateful and acknowledged and delivered
and watching with me this new vision.

Smoke. Replaced.
With joy. In light.
Souls. In flight.

When I come back to the video to watch again
the next day, I see it. Billowing clouds of color and
whimsy replace clouds of ash that have repeated in
memory for a decade. Surprise of delight replaces
shock of fear, confusion. A crystalline day reclaims
sweetness.

In remembrance.

In memory.

In living. Wonder.

(Totally 100% recommend watching the video. Scan the QR code or web search "Sony colorful bouncing balls." Turn up your volume, and float.)

DAY 27
A Letter to Innocence: Snapshot of a Beginning at the Eve of an End

Beginnings and endings

I hear so many stories of beginnings from people who were witness to the 9/11 attacks in New York. A friend I met recently arrived the day before in a moving truck. Another got sober the day before, conceived her child two days after. I arrived on August 22nd. Grad school started on September 10th. And the stories continue. Was it a season of beginnings? Or was it a heyday of creation, creativity always beginning at something?

When I went to grad school, I didn't do it alone. I often referred to it as church camp without God. Our class bonded immediately, the actors, directors, and playwrights, the teachers, the staff, the admin. Orientation week settled us into the city, and on the first day of classes and the first night of taping at *Inside the Actors Studio*, we laughed as Bruce Willis told us he had saved the world seventeen times in his movies. We were twelve hours away from a plane hitting Tower One two miles south.

Light framed

We would have gotten to know each other deeply in the ways we exposed ourselves in our work anyway. But the events of 9/11 sped that up in a ghastly precursor that blew open the doors, ready or not. Being creatives, the only way to survive was to work. Being theatre folk, we created by being a group, opening up and diving together into the places in us that would be freed.

A decade later, Rhea MacCallum, my fellow classmate and award-winning playwright, posted a letter on Facebook to Cohort 8 of the Actor's Studio Drama School. She captures our excited sense of "purpose, potential, community, security, and hope." Her images are so clear, her memory so dear in framing our hopes and courage and leaps of faith and people who supported us to be there taking them, that they tell a story of light I wished for as I wrote this material.

With great thanks to Rhea, I invite you into the picture of light that brings to life those days in the beginning, as the end of what we knew of our world was beginning, too. Rhea's recall is so profound, she remembered nearly every person and wrote one line about what she remembered about each. I can't include them all here, but for their vitality, for the essence of a life moment distilled to one line, I included a few.

Dear Cohort VIII,

Ten years ago today we introduced ourselves to each other. So much of our orientation week bounces around like a fiery comet trapped in my brain. As we filtered into Tishman we were continuously instructed to 'come forward, move to the center, leave no empty spaces' and the mostly vacant auditorium vibrated with our exuberant energy.

That day, that first day, we met James Lipton. We were told that our talent was as recognizable as spotting your sister in a crowd. We were told playwrights don't hug and most of us promptly decided that we would be the exception. Then we got up, one by one, alternating sides of the room and introduced ourselves. Our name, our track, where we were from, what brought us here.

A few weeks later, after the planes hit, after the towers fell, after walking from hospital to hospital looking to give blood, after surviving world-altering events, we gathered again, a bonded unit, for a workshop led by Teresa T. Our homework was to bring a personal object, something of great significance to us. Our classwork was to share with each other what we brought and why we chose it, in three sentences.

Ten years later, our orientation week and personal object workshop have become bits of memory strung together in a not so linear fashion. When I look back at our grad school experience, and think of it fondly, these two events emerge as moments in which I was filled with a sense of purpose, potential, community, security, and hope.

This is what I remember...

Henry's map of NYC.

CiCi with her boyfriend's wallet filled with cash he'd earned over the summer.

Mika and her father's watch.

Theo, who made a number of people sit up and take notice when he said he applied to grad school because "he always felt like a fraud."

Nando, who sat next to me and already had an MA from NYU.

Rochelle, who thought life stopped after 25.

Maria, who was still holding onto Izzy's ring when she walked away to go to the restroom, leaving a nervous-looking Izzy alone.

Amanda, who tugged at our heartstrings as she spoke of her janitor father who worked extra shifts so she could pursue her dream and made us all chuckle when she brought in a strawberry air freshener that survived, what was it, seven? car accidents.

I remember my mother being comforted to hear that I was studying playwriting with a Teeter (my grandmother's maiden name) and a Stevenson (her maiden name) taught by a Laura (my sister's name). She wasn't normally one to view the world through cosmic signs, but she made an exception. She felt I was in the right place, at the right time, with the right people.

Try as I might, I don't remember everyone from those early days. Isn't the brain a funny thing? Why do I remember, so vividly, Nikki Anderson, who I spoke to once, once in my life, but not so many others? And as for the accuracy of my memory, well, only you can tell me how well I did.

I just wanted to let you know that I'm thinking of you, as I do every year when it gets to be about this time. And when I think of you, when I think of us, as we were in these days, I smile through the tears.

Lots of love,
Rhea

DAY 28
Prayer Man

In 2006, I had a series of readings with Robin, the psychic medium who confirmed what another person had suggested were "souls in my field." It was also suggested that the serious, seemingly impossible-to-heal problem I was having with my skin was directly related. The following is an excerpt from one of our readings.

R: How are you feeling?

P: I guess it comes in waves . . . . I'm really, really itchy. I mean, that is there all the time at different parts of my body. But in terms of anxiety, like when I saw you guys last, I was a wreck, so anxious from all of the itching. In the past week or so I've gotten some calmness but I still get pretty anxious sometimes when the itching is bad.

R: Yeah, I would think so.

P: It's bad. I look like I have the chicken pox.

R: I'm so sorry that's happening to you. What did the doctor say?

P: I went to the homeopath, and he's just checking it out. It's just the beginning. I didn't go to the regular doctor because they haven't tended to help me and also every time I take something for it, it seems to get worse.

R: Yeah.

P: And a couple of things have crossed my mind, like today I noticed I was scratching and scratching and scratching and the skin I just leave skin behind like dust, and I saw it falling to the ground and I thought, "It's like ash." And then I thought, "Oh, it's like *ash*. It's the working title of my book, *Voices from the Ash*.

R: Yeah, well, that is what I feel vividly, is that this is about that, and I guess you have a predisposition to it anyway but this is really intense. So I am hearing to proceed in reading, so I'm gonna go ahead and connect with your soul and say a prayer and then just see where we go and take it from your questions and just see what happens, okay?

P: Okay.

R: The voices from the ash are telling me we need to clear your system so that you're not carrying it through your physical body but you're downloading their experience through your higher states of consciousness, so that—there it goes. It's shifting.

Now I seem to be inside either a room or an airplane, and I just heard "Airplane is it." And I'm seeing people in their seats and they're not very alarmed. There's people walking up and down the aisle, but there's no disturbances, no energetic knowing that harm is about to descend on people, so the lack of awareness is really permeating this vision, the innocence of this vision is coming in, and then I'm seeing an individual begin to make some sort of an attack, whether it's someone taking someone else hostage or a verbal exchange, you know getting people to understand what's about to happen. And there's a lot of emotional response here.

You've picked up on the emotional charge of the people at this time. I'm hearing it's a byproduct of the people in the plane. I'm hearing there's eight people here that are somehow involved with you that are running your energy. I've got to find a way to communicate here.

Okay I'm going back up into the vision of the airplane. And there does seem to be an individual who is remaining calm. Very calm. I'm gonna see if I can bring some of that energy into your field. And I'm hearing that approach isn't working either. So I'm just gonna stay with that individual and just see if there's um—okay let's try tithing that calmness out to the group and bring them in this pre-death experience to—there it goes, it's shifting. What are you feeling in your body right now?

P: I feel like calmness washing over my skin, not just over my muscles or something but over my skin.

R: Good. Your energy became your own again. Now, "transmutation device is deficient." What the heck does that mean? Is that in Pema or is that in the soul group? I'm getting soul group, Beloved. Okay. So, what is a transmutation device?

P: I keep thinking that I'm the transmutation device, if I'm trying to transmute their voices out from my body and from this experience into, you know, existence. I feel like, my biggest question is, "How do I train myself through this?"

R: Yeah, I think this is exactly it. And that's what I've been feeling that this story is about your experience with these people, it's not—like I think before you were thinking about just channeling them, but what you're having to go through to be their transmutation device so their voices can be heard I think is just as important. Because I think as people it just feels like it's really important that in the process of all humans waking up we all become more telepathic, we all become more sensitive, so how does one cope with that?

P: Right.

R: Okay . . . . And now I'm back up on the airplane and the man who was calm had the tools to remain calm in a crisis. He had the metaphysical tools, he had the knowing, he had the trust, that you know, no harm would come to him, you know, even if he blew up in an airplane, he trusted that everything was happening for a divine purpose and he was equipped for the danger, if you will. So okay let's see, he says he wants to speak a little bit more here. I'm feeling that he might have been either of Indian descent, although I feel he may have been American as well, so he may have been both, or he had studied [different methods used in India as] tools of staying calm.

It seems like this person had something red. And I'm also hearing he had prayer beads. And the power of prayer is very strong here. He's saying that he was praying that their voices would be heard. He was praying for peace. He was praying that there would be a transmutation device who would hear him beyond death and be his voice and speak this information that's coming through. And he's saying it's not about religion it's not about that separate thinking. There you go, you're taking it in. What's happening with you?

P: When you were talking I had chills all over, I have tears in my eyes, like I'm here, like I hear him, like, "Oh, it's me."

R: Yeah. Yeah. I feel like tonight is really about connecting with this particular soul, because he knew that there was no other means of communication but to go directly to his soul, to his high self, and put out a signal from that high place, that he would be heard beyond the grave, that he knew the eternal.

P: I feel that so much I just keep getting chills all over my body, and I feel really close to him.

R: Yeah. He feels really close to you too. My feeling is that there was almost like a moment of impact where your souls connected. And I'm hearing prior to death is strong, so his conscious attempt to reach out to someone and your willingness in your ability to pick it up feels very, very strong to me.

P: I have chills again.

R: Yeah. So I'm feeling like he may have actually had some kind of a vision, or a knowing; he's saying it wasn't a vision, it was a knowing just prior to the impact that caused his death, he knew someone had conn—he knew he had connected, and he's saying when that happened, his soul purpose was fulfilled, and what you do with it, Beloved, is up to you.

DAY 29
One

Mind's eye

It is a Saturday. I pin my voice recorder mic to my jacket and lie down on the crest of a grassy hill. View of the ocean. University buildings behind me. Weekend courses in session and people around, but no one close. I plan on talking to myself about some very off-the-wall stuff, so a spot with no one close by is important. No more futzing. Final falsetto trill shakes the nerves.

I close my eyes.

I breathe. I meditate. Almost immediately, I see a woman in my mind's eye. She wears white denim pants, a white sweater, loosely knit, and a slender belt on her jeans. She is barefoot. She stands there looking like she is waiting for something. Of course, I figure I am making her up . . . so she waits. Finally I say, "Nancy? Are you here?"

The image smiles.

Ohmigod.

Reach my story

An image of a da Vinci drawing pops into my head, the *Vitruvian Man* in the circle. I ask her if that is for me and she nods.

Weird. Okay, continuing. I notice a few other things about her out loud, like she's not wearing glasses; she's standing, not sitting. I get this feeling that she's still waiting, and that something is working. So, I launch in.

"Can you tell me why I'm here today?"

She has been nodding up to now. I tell her, "You can speak to me. I would like to hear your voice."

Nancy speaks. I can't hear her, but I am reading her lips as she speaks slowly. "I want you to tell my story. I want you to reach my story to the world and all who will listen to it."

She is nodding and saying thank you. I'm watching her mouth move, turning into communication, and I get a rush of wonder.

Rush of wonder

"Thank you, Nancy. I'm listening and I'm watching. What is your story? What do you want me to say for you, on behalf of you? I feel an urgency in my chest and my heart right now, kind of a welling up."

Nancy's nodding is vigorous now. Yes yes yes. She is sitting now. Her feet are together, her hands on her knees, which are together. She is sitting up tall and leaning forward toward me. "I want you to share and to pray. Pray for yourselves, for your welfare. Pray that your welfare will be in good hands."

Immediately my heart plunks a minor key. "Pray?" I ask her. "Is that what you said?" I am definitely not making this up. I'd had my falling out with religion as a queer teen passing for good girl in the church pews. Praying didn't work for me.

She nods again. "The most important word is 'pray,'" she says.

"Who should we pray to?" I ask.

"Your god, your nature. Your spirit. Just be quiet." Nancy is closing her eyes in stillness. She brings her hands together in front of her chest, drops her head in a bow and says, "Just be still." She takes a deep breath. "Go inward."

Letting the light shine

At this point as I lay on the blanket, I feel an odd stillness in my feet, as if they are sleeping—not tingling, but taking a nap and I don't want to disturb them. I tell Nancy this and she nods. Then they do begin to tingle, but only from the top of the arch to the underside. The tingling intensifies and another image enters my head, yet another plunk in a minor key. But I've come this far. I decide to go for it.

"Nancy, do you mean Jesus?"

She nods.

This is not the hip, New Age experience I am expecting. I follow the image she gives me, the Jesus in my feet, and her hands placed together in prayer, and continue speaking, "Letting the light shine through the crucifix holes of the palms as they're placed together."

She nods. My feet begin to buzz.

"Is Jesus present?" I ask.

She nods again.

"Did you pray to Jesus?"

Nancy is crying. She was very afraid before she died. She prayed. I am seeing her on her knees. She was sending her daughters love. She was wishing they could hear her, that she could be with them, wishing that the distance between them in that moment was not so impossibly far. Nancy is crying. Her face is wet with tears. She stands up and looks out a window of the World Trade Center.

"You should love your daughters fiercely," she says, "but tenderly. Bless them because they are not only your daughters in flesh but they are your connection, your people. You reach far forward and far back in time together. You miss them not only when they die but when you die. You love them as family forever."

One

Nancy is now on her knees with her hands together. "Tell my daughters to take the best of me and send it along through their lineage. Let them know they carry the lineage of light. It is our lineage to spread this light, to share it, in being this family of light, this soul family that started long before our human flesh. Remember what begins with you ends with you, and connects in you, and together, you are whole and one, and you may walk on the earth as one, together in light, with Jesus, who is light, beaming through him. One."

The words come in a rush. When they are over, the image of Nancy is quiet, still kneeling.

I am quiet too. Then, "Nancy," I say. "Do you have more to say?"

She shakes her head. I thank her. And then I open my eyes. The sky is as blue as when I started. A bird circles overhead. I am a little afraid to notice myself now that I am back in real time again. Did all of that just happen? I press a button on my digital recorder and hear the words again. I press stop.

It did.

I give thanks, fold my blanket, and drive away.

DAY 30
Vitruvian Man

On my first research trip back to New York City, I planned to go to the reading of the names at Ground Zero on 9/11. Before my research trips began, in all of the times I'd traveled to New York, I had been too afraid of my feelings to go to Ground Zero. Once, I got close, but denial is a powerful thing: I saw tarps and fences and didn't recognize what I was looking at.

On 9/11/2007, I was having breakfast at a smoothie shop and collecting my nerves before heading down to the ceremony to listen to the reading of the names. From my tiny table, I saw at the cashier counter a table tent ad with a picture of da Vinci's Vitruvian Man superimposed over a lemon.

I remembered the meditation I'd had with Nancy that opened with the Vitruvian Man image and had to remind myself to breathe. I didn't understand why seeing it at a smoothie shop was particularly profound. Maybe I was on the right track, emotionally, going to the names ceremony for the first time.

When I got there, people were lining sidewalks around the sunken area that was formerly the World Trade Center. It was a hole in the city surrounded by buildings, and the sunken area was staged with chairs and a lectern and speakers for the ceremony. I leaned against a building next to a cop directing foot traffic and took in people's quiet sobriety.

Then, I saw it. High on a crane boom, a distance behind the proceedings, in the gray sky, was a bright yellow lemon-shaped load block, the part of the crane that the hook attaches to.

Vitruvian Man. Lemon. They had stood out as weird when I had seen them out of context, in my meditation with Nancy and at the smoothie shop. Now taking note of them, accepting their context, made me feel less alone, not so scared to feel. Not as irrational as I'd been feeling this whole journey that had turned metaphysical when someone introduced the idea of souls in my field.

DAY 31
Setting It Free

Shift in the atmosphere

Today: I am making muffins. I am driving to Portland from San Francisco. I am getting a pedicure because I'm going to a party where there will be pretty girls in pretty dresses and I want to be one of them. Today I am fighting with my boyfriend. I am feeling like a woman. I am arriving home.

Ten years ago today: I was sitting in a café in NYC, across the street from my new grad school, writing a letter to a friend from days and cities gone past. I was attending our first taping of *Inside the Actors Studio* and riding the subway with excited classmates to Brooklyn after the show. The car was nearly empty. We were singing show tunes and I was imagining a new play.

Eight weeks ago, today: It's early July and I have plans to spend the tenth anniversary of 9/11 in New York. My stories will be written by then. The circle that opened there in 2001 will find some bit closure on the anniversary. My pilgrimage will culminate in glorious celebration of the city on the *Wonder Walk*, TheSecretCity.org's annual fourteen-hour art and performance walk from the northern tip of Manhattan to the Brooklyn Bridge. There will be much to marvel at and much wonder to behold in a city still healing from its loss.

I have plans to spend August writing in Santa Barbara. I will miss a big portion of my best friend's pregnancy. But the project is necessary. It's a healing and a calling. I'll squeeze in as much time as possible to make up my absence when I get back and before I go.

I have plans to spend my late-July birthday with my boyfriend. He's taking vacation from work to come visit for the week and make it special.

But in the morning, I get a call from my friend in Santa Barbara who says a dear friend and mentor, Max, has died suddenly. I feel shocked and sad and unhinged. I feel out of control of my fate in the universe. After a moment of thought, I set about making it to his funeral, against all good judgment regarding time and distance. But I am resourceful. I have spent a life organizing on the fly like this. I can make it happen. I can begin my stay in Santa Barbara early, after the funeral.

In the course of twenty-four hours, I hire cat sitters to move into my apartment, and cancel my boyfriend's week-long plan to visit for my birthday. "I have to be at the funeral," I tell him. Max was important to me. He sent the last email in our correspondence on the morning of the day he died. We were making plans to see each other a few weeks later. We were going to share ideas. We had plans.

When I call to cancel on my best friend, she asks, "When will you be back?"

"I'm just not sure," I tell her.

And she says, with some futility in her voice, "My baby shower is September 11." My best friend tried for five years to get pregnant. Now, she is living her dream, due in November, twins.

I in my spin say, "September 11?" while I'm thinking, "Does she not know me?" And I say, "It's the tenth anniversary!" And I can hear the loss in her silence, the shock in it, and I can feel the shock in my reply. I can feel the impossibility of it. My best friend. Living her dream. I am not there for it. This dream of my own—these stories that have been trying to get written, too intense to ignore, finally finding expression, ending on September 11 in New York, my dream against the grain of her dream, impossible fusion.

I have to go the next morning, early. Which means no time to come over and say good-bye. I tell myself she'll understand. It's a funeral. I have to go.

I tell her. She is hurt. She is anything but understanding.

The spin

My arrangements slide into place strangely easily. But by the time I finish making them, I am no less unhinged.

I call my friend, Lisa. "Can you help me?" I ask. "I have to talk this out, will you listen?"

Lisa agrees. And when I've spun my wheels to exhaustion, she quietly asks me, "Why did you come to me with this?"

I ask her for the reason behind her question and she says, "We go to different people with our problems when we want to hear particular answers. What kind of answer are you looking for from me?"

And I say, "Whatever there is for you to say." And she proceeds—softly, with the precision of a friend whose love observes and waits for the right time to share—to put words to the moments over our years where I have prioritized death over life, even when we were young and still figuring things out.

And I see that I have chosen death over life. I have chucked my plans that are full of life, full of people I love and who love me back, to be present at a funeral that, while very dear, is a two-hour memorial, for a friend who is gone.

Overtaken

I sit with that. I get it. It is part of the uneasiness I have been feeling in my spin. I just haven't been able to grasp it.

And Lisa, as my friend for years, quietly testifies that it is not the first time. That this impulse in me has had impact on my relationships in the past. And I for the first time am seeing them in this context. Seeing my leaving in this light. Seeing my running toward loss against the presence of love, right here, right now.

I feel the gravity of that. I feel like heaps of shit. I have made a very big mistake. For decades. But for the first time in two days, I am calm.

I hang up with Lisa. I hold my head in my hands. I begin the effort of patching back together what I have undone.

9/11, and every year since, remembered

On 9/11/01, after I saw what I saw, heard what I heard, I called one household, holding two of my core. Laura grumbled out of bed to turn on the TV at Suzy's urgent demand. Suzy was on the phone with me. We connected, I shared phone numbers, we told each other we loved each other, and I went back out into the city. In California, Laura and Suzy watched the news play and replay the now-iconic videos of the attacks.

Since that day, Laura has become a mom. In observation of September 11, 2001, her remembrance honors the lost and the left behind with the love and devastation of motherhood, possibility, impossibility and peace.

Setting it free: My poem 10 years later

By Laura Smith

It's 1 a.m. and I can't sleep.

4 a.m. on the East Coast.

I walk to the kitchen to get a glass of water.

Place a finger beneath my child's nose to make sure
    they're still breathing.

Can't shake the feeling that something's not right.

4 a.m. on the East Coast, 9/11/11.

Ten years ago, thousands of people still sleeping in
    their beds.

Deep in their peaceful REM cycles on a crisp fall morning

Unaware that they'll leave their homes for the last time
    that day.

Unaware that something is just not right.

What did those people leave undone that day?

Lawns unmowed, fish unfed, dishes unwashed?

Last month's electric bill past due and fallen between the
    desk & the wall.

Who were they and how did they live, how did they love?

And how do the people they loved continue to go on
    without them?

And what, I must ask, what in their names, have
WE done?
How many times has a mother in Bagdad felt every
day for the past 10 years
What the mothers of this nation felt on that one
terrible day?
Waiting to hear if her children have survived a
battle zone.
Waiting for someone to walk through the door who
will never come home again.

And what, if anything, do we still need to do, 10 years
later?
Is it even possible for us to choose peace?
Is it possible for us to rise up and say that we were
wrong?
Can we ever convince our leaders that a war on fear
Is like smacking a kid to teach them that hitting is
wrong.

It's 2 a.m. and I might sleep.
I might dream of the stories of my friends who have
started to share
Where they were and what they saw and what they
remember.

In the sharing of memories and emotions, we breathe it
out, and we honor it.
We honor the dead and the grieving and the wounded by
sharing and setting it free.

SEPTEMBER 11, 2011
Memory to Light

The Dream

It's August. I'm in Santa Barbara. I am writing a story a day to give grief its due. From August 11 to September 11, I am airing out grief, telling stories of trauma in my life that came before 9/11, and telling my stories of what I saw that day in New York.

I have come to believe, at the time I begin this project, that giving space to grief by telling its stories is the process of transformation. I want to feel what happens when we—I—witness, allow, feel, open, and heal collectively from the losses we share. I want to let grief move and make space for a self and a life my tucked-away sorrows can't see yet. I want to feel others. I want to connect, bridge the waterways between my island and the rest of my life, and know I am not alone.

Light

It's September 11, 2011. Yesterday and the day before, I spend in my car, driving to the final chapter.

I arrive. I help set up tables in prep for a gathering. I spend the morning crying while listening to radio interviews and audio files played in honor of the tenth anniversary. I wipe my face of tears while watching videos that are traveling around the internet. I post a poem, remembering what has come and what has gone. And, soon, I choose a time to let my crying cease, let the grief be fully felt, and then recede, let light come back into the day, as I get dressed for my best friend's baby shower.

There are new twins being celebrated today, as we remember the Twin Towers that fell. There are new lives coming into focus today, as we remember the lives that extinguished those years ago. There is collective love today, gathering around parents and two little humans finding their way into the world, as our country forms community in remembering those we lost. There is life here.

There is life in the pain. It's why it hurts.

There is life in the grief, in astonishing volume.

There is spirit past the ashes, and love and love and love.

There is light here.

EPILOGUE

Finding meaning

After David died, I was confounded. He was such a vivid and integral part of me, I couldn't understand how that relationship was supposed to just end. I was here. My feet were still shaped like his had been, and carried my sturdy body in the same way his had carried his exact frame. What I understood about my life, it all led back to David. To know him was to know me, to know me was to know my brother, and now he was . . . gone? My constant query became, "How do I have a relationship with a dead person?"

I fostered this question for three decades. In the early years, I nearly stopped speaking. I began deeply listening, to people's words but also to their tone and the space between words. I began to imagine that everything is animated, like my love for my brother remained animated, with its own intelligence which refused to die. I listened for anything that any room, any tree or ant or hillside might have to say. I got so good at listening and interpreting meaning, I became a ghostwriter in my career, a voice for other people, a channel for others' voices.

In the years after 9/11, when my suppressed feelings were struggling out through panic and anxiety and a stress-related skin condition, and then two unrelated people told me about souls in my field, I was confounded. "Why me? I don't speak that language. I don't fully believe those two people aren't putting me on. This is incredibly sensitive material that affects loved ones intimately. What do I do with this information?"

Then I felt the physical sensation of relief and light when Robin channeled the soul collective that first time, and it was enough to get me asking questions and listening, for whatever there was to be said, by whoever was there to say it. What started as a physical journey to heal my skin turned into a metaphysical journey that taught me about connection: that it doesn't stop when the body stops, that our love and our loves continue.

I am no longer confounded. I don't know everything there is to know about mediumship or counseling grief, or even how to recognize each opportunity to take the deep breaths and move into feeling every time grief shows up for me to feel. I do know that if grief is another country, spirit is another language. Our own spirit guiding the emotional immune system; synchronicity and connected dots and messages in the animated world; a higher power; an order in the universe; spirits no longer in body, who are present with love and care—come together in a living lexicon, connecting me and anyone willing to hear it to this web of life we share. I am never alone. We are never alone. When I listen, I can hear love calling me, and others, in voices I once thought were gone.

Floating on the breeze

Forty-eight hours before I wrote this epilogue, I was in a personal crisis of historical triggers and deep upheaval. In preparing to write about connection, I had become trapped in a painful disconnection with a loved one, while on vacation. My bereft, deserted, terrified feeling called back to the loss of my mother so specifically, I felt like a child, powerless and alone.

In response, I made last-minute arrangements to travel to a dear friend's house in another city. Lisa and I had been connected all through the pandemic, and when my dad died, four days after I got vaccinated, she held me the moment I was cleared to travel. Two months later, nearly as suddenly, Lisa's sweet mama died and we cried together miles apart day by day. Susan was a personification of love. Her heart reached out to every one of Lisa's friends, to her community, to people of the world through her lifelong growth and curiosity and endearing way she connected with those around her. She loved her family with her sheltering heart and her encouraging belief in each of them. After Susan passed, Lisa repeated in our conversations, like a prayer sometimes, the story of some of Susan's last words. She said, "I'm a little feather, floating on the breeze." Her words were a sweet balm when she said them. Now that Susan had gone, they felt like a gift.

My travel was set after a late night and full morning of arrangements. I would arrive at Lisa's by evening. I took a big breath to change channels and pack, feel some relief. I was wound up in the way I was leaving, and in the haunted way it dropped me and left me in my motherless early years. I put in my headset and opened the chill music station on my phone to help regulate my nervous system. Since I had last seen this station, the company had animated the onscreen image of it. What was once a static circle behind a geometric shape was now a transparent sphere in which a white feather floated in rotation. I began to cry. I felt motherhood sweep in and hold me. And I finally put it together that I'd be seeing Lisa for the first time since her mom had passed. I would be able to hug Lisa in her loss. And I'd be able to bring Susan with me in the hug.

I felt the peaceful feeling that comes of recognizing spirit language. I no longer felt alone. In the timeliest of moments, I felt the deep love Susan shared while she was alive. It was as if she knew I was headed to see her beloved daughter, and, true to her nature, floated precisely into that opening to give her love to both of us.

Connection

When I get quiet, I hear this directive I hope to keep remembering—I hope you'll remember it with me: Acknowledge grief. Listen for spirit. It's all here for us, in each other, in ourselves.

ACKNOWLEDGMENTS

In twenty years, many people have breathed life into this book. For this web of humanity, I am grateful. Thanks to:

Everyone who read along and shared stories and encouragement in the original 2011 grief-sharing project on StoryCharmer.com; and the kind folks who allowed those stories to be included in the "Collective's voice."

All the folks who generously allowed me to interview them.

ASDS cohort eight, especially the folks who walked with me that day, made it through class together that morning, and talked with me in my quests in the years that followed: Bi Ngo, Nichol Alexander, Matt Olmos, Mary Flanagan, Rhea MacCallum, Jonathan Howle, Michael Raimondi, A. Sayeeda Clark. Judith Grodowitz, Laura Maria Censabella. In loving memory, Elizabeth Kemp.

Britt Andreatta, from an emotional beginning twenty years ago to the end she always envisioned, encouraged, and helped me to materialize.

Suzanne Giesemann, for her immediate support and open heart. I looked for her for decades, and suddenly, there she was.

Jenefer Angell, Wanna Johansson, and Ellie Sipila, for their vision, talent and gracious co-creating. Morgan Krehbiel for her steady direction and print design.

Leah Finch, collaboration station, always open.

Robin Alexis, seer, supporter, community builder.

Regina Perata, Gina Diaz, and C & G, family found.

For seeing me off to NYC with love and belief in me: Duane Daniels, Kim Higuchi, Michelle Skoor, Wendy Tienken, Alison Mitsuhashi, Jane Chandler, and Miriam Geller.

For receiving me with home and heart: Roseanne Ciparick.

Suzy Schutz, who always answers when I call, and finds me when I can't find my way; who answered the call that day and talked my grandma through it.

Laura Smith, who witnessed from home and has witnessed all these years.

Jose Rivera, Adena Rivera-Dundas, and Teo Rivera-Dundas caught me as I slid.

Then, Steven Lovelace, Gary Clark, Kara Powis, and Kate Tierney did, too.

Barbara Pantuso and Miles Barger hosted me on research and writing trips.

In a fog of phenomena and feeling, Julie Daley gave traction to my overwhelming ideas.

Tifanie McQueen, Eric Vollmer, Poorna Jagannathan, Matthew Taviannini, and Gunther Oakey cheer-led early versions of this project in conversations and public audiences.

Laura S. talked spirit with me and tracked lost loved ones in wonder and continual discovery.

Celebrate Life Spiritualist Church in San Francisco, James Bae, Drew Vogt, and Karyn Crisis validated my experiences and helped teach me a new language.

The books of authors Carmen Maria Machado and Natalie Singer, as well as Lidia Yuknavitch and the authors and writers at Corporeal Writing gave me permission to play with literary form.

Elaine Huang's and Helene Goode's compassion, depth and precision have expanded my understanding every time we've met.

Tania Israel and Lisa Slavid each grieved with me, encouraged me, and hosted me as I wrote this, ten years ago when it began and, miraculously, again at its end. Their wisdom and support lives in every page.

Skies of thanks to:

Eric Kome, who reached through time to ask: Yes, I am okay.

Elizabeth Ceras, whose energy lit a path through the writing.

Elaine Gale, who reveled and read with enthusiasm.

A most special thanks to Lucia Matioli for inspiring the love, confidence, and courage to keep coming back to give this story its due. And to Chelsea Brunetti, my fellow builder of bridges from heart to persistence.

Thank you: Floyd Rocker, Chris Sneathen and Kiana Sneathen, Claudia Arnett, Monica Lenches, Dana Campagna. Michelle Miller. Missy Shepard Bajadek for remembering every year. And Teresa Fannuchi, in loving memory and giddy celebration.

And, thanks to my family, who bear the weight of our shared losses the best we know how, together and apart, with more love and practice all the time.

It's hard to express in a line of thanks how much I love, miss and appreciate my mentor garden, but I hope these pages can: David, Joyce, Christiaan, Gabriel, Gabe, Roy, MK and Talia, Orin and Lucille, Mike and Rainey, Nellie Mae, Lonnie, Dad, Tommy—you've taught me a life with grief hurts, but grows rich with new language, senses, fullness, love.

ABOUT THE AUTHOR

Pema Rocker helps people connect—to self, to others, and to the magic inherent in creating and relating. Creativity coach and intuitive guide, she has helped Grammys get won, businesses get launched, and stories get told.

The journey in this book led Pema to investigate expressions of energy in its many mutable forms. "Listening-extra" is what she calls her heightened tracking of stories, circumstances, and extrasensory experience that connects-the-dots to new understanding, strategy, or simply reflecting people's deep inner knowing.

Since 2008, she has been a ghost writer and interviewer for thought leaders, and has created and curated magazines for Queer and spiritual communities. She leads groups to connect through the power of story, and guides individuals through transition and creative blocks. Pema lives in Portland, Oregon. This is her first book.

Websites: PemaRocker.com and StoryCharmer.com

RESOURCES

This book brings up the notion of developing a "skill in grief." Grief is such a blow, sometimes we can only wonder, "What now?" And, "How?" What happens next, for ourselves individually and in collective? It also explores the surprise of sensing relationship beyond death, and developing a language to understand it. Here is a short list of resources to give you some ideas of what to search on your own, in your locality, affinity, and topic areas. There are in-person and virtual gatherings, books, links to online resource lists, and social media offerings. As always, if you like a resource, dive into its hashtags, references, and podcast notes to find their influences and expand your net.

For an ongoing list of crowd-sourced resources, and to share what's helped you, visit:

@Ash.and.Spirit on Instagram
www.instagram.com/ash.and.spirit/

We learn from each other. Please share what has helped you.

Peer & Professional Support

▶ **12-Step Recovery Programs**

Twelve-step fellowships use the strength of community, the principles of the program and, in the case of those founded by Alcoholics Anonymous (AA), a spiritual guidance personal to each individual, to help peers grow through and beyond addiction in their lives. Many fellowships include literature and meetings that address and discuss grief, trauma, and loss, both present and past, such as Al-Anon and Adult Children of Alcoholics (ACA)/Dysfunctional Families. You can find information online and in person around the globe at their websites.

ACA *www.adultchildren.org*

From their website: "Adult Children of Alcoholics (ACA)/Dysfunctional Families is a Twelve Step, Twelve Tradition program of people who grew up in dysfunctional homes. We meet to share our experience of growing up in an environment where abuse, neglect and trauma infected us. This affects us today and influences how we deal with all aspects of our lives. ACA provides a safe, nonjudgmental environment that allows us to grieve our childhoods and conduct an honest inventory of ourselves and our family—so we may (i) identify and heal core trauma, (ii) experience freedom from shame and abandonment, and (iii) become our own loving parents."

Al-Anon *www.al-anon.org*

From their website: "Al-Anon Family Groups meet in over 130 countries to help families and friends of problem drinkers recover from the impacts of a loved one's drinking. Members help each other by practicing the Twelve Steps of Alcoholics Anonymous themselves, by welcoming and giving comfort to families of alcoholics, and by giving understanding and encouragement to the alcoholic. The assurance of anonymity is essential to Al-Anon's efforts to help more families and friends of alcoholics."

▶ **The Dougy Center for Grieving Children and Families**
www.dougy.org

In addition to in-person support for young grievers and their families, they also have video training programs to become peer group facilitators. Dougy Center is located in Portland, Oregon.

▶ **Dove Lewis Pet Hospital**
www.dovelewis.org/pet-owners/pet-loss-support

Virtual and in-person pet loss support groups, hosted by a local pet hospital in Portland, Oregon. There is a grief support circle for pet loss, and an annual memorial service for pet parents to honor pets who have passed. Check your area for similar offerings.

▶ **Helping Parents Heal**
www.helpingparentsheal.org

"Helping Parents Heal is a non-profit organization dedicated to assisting parents whose children have passed. Through support and resources, we aspire to help individuals become 'Shining Light Parents,' meaning a shift from a state of emotional heaviness to hopefulness and greater peace of mind. HPH goes a step beyond other groups by allowing the open discussion of spiritual experiences and afterlife evidence in a non-dogmatic way. HPH welcomes everyone regardless of religious or non-religious background and encourages open dialog." They also have affinity groups on the site for siblings and fathers, called "Helping Siblings Heal" and "Helping Fathers Heal."

▶ **The Hospice Foundation of America**
hospicefoundation.org/Grief-(1)

"HFA is a trusted source of information on end of life, hospice care and grief." The Grief Resources pages of their website list many opportunities for connection, support, and information.

Intersectional, Affinity, and Activity Groups

Grief is universal. But it's also intimate. Sometimes you just don't have bandwidth to feel othered while grieving. It can bring up an ongoing feeling of loss that can outweigh intended support. You can find affinity groups online and possibly in your area by narrowing your searches by affinity. Additionally, there are activity groups and courses that make space for grief in the making of their content. Consider what feels good to engage, and explore offerings that hold a whole person into account while crafting or connecting or building.

▶ **LGBTQIA+ centers**
Centerlink LGBTQ Center Directory – www.lgbtqcenters.org /LGBTCenters

▶ **Black and Brown Good Grief**
www.thenewnormalcharity.com/meetings/black-and-brown -good-grief

". . . [P]eer to peer support meeting and safe space for black and brown grievers. Black and Brown Good Grief allows a person to grieve acknowledging the nuances of their heritage and culture while still being a person grieving someone. Black and Brown Good Grief was started by black and brown attendees and continues to be run and hosted this way."

▶ **GriefKnits Support Group**
by the Drew Michael Taylor Foundation – drewmichaeltaylor.org/resources

Check your locality for crafting support groups in your area. From the Drew Michael Taylor Foundation website: "Knitting has shown positive mental health benefits for grievers. Come and meet others who are grieving the death of a loved one and learn to knit too . . . or bring another craft project! Not crafty? That's okay too. You are welcome to gather with us for conversation and fellowship."

▶ **"Interfaith, interspiritual, interspecies"**
Compassion Consortium – www.compassionconsortium.org/about

"The Compassion Consortium is a non-sectarian center. We offer well-being resources, spiritual guidance, support, and community fellowship to Vegans, Vegetarians, animal rights activists, animal lovers, and all humans who care about and advocate for animals and the planet. . . . The Consortium also hosts additional events, classes, and interest groups (such as the Book and Film Events), and offers services including pastoral counseling and companion animal grief counseling, animal chaplaincy, and animal Reiki. Our website itself is an ever-renewing resource for information about inclusive spirituality. The Compassion Consortium celebrates diversity and operates with an inviolable anti-racist and anti-speciesist ethic. While our ministry is global, we are based in New York City, where we are organized as a non-for-profit religious corporation."

▶ **Intergenerational immigrant families**
MESO – www.mesocommunity.com

"We generate connections and possibilities for our immigrant communities. We address challenges of caregiving, unspoken loss, and grief with culturally informed workshops, online courses, and 1:1 or community grief support. In creating compassionate spaces and offering resources, we aim to inform, cultivate capacity, and support any immigrant family in one of the most vulnerable and important times of life."

▶ **Surfers and Nature Lovers**
Waves of Grief – www.wavesofgrief.org/about

". . . [C]reating new meaningful experiences in integrated grief in at the ocean's shores. The hope is that those who opt into Waves of Grief™ create their own sustainable therapeutic process in nature that is held and supported by the community fostered in the program. . . . [Established] to reduce loneliness and isolation in grief during COVID-19's early, most traumatic days."

▶ **Teens and young adults**
collegeeducated.com/resources/grief-resources-for-college -students

▶ **Traumatic injury**
Trauma Survivors Network – www.traumasurvivorsnetwork.org

"We are a community of patients and survivors looking to connect with one another and rebuild their lives after a serious injury."

▶ **Veterans**
Tragedy Assistance Program for Survivors – www.TAPS.org

Comprehensive resources for those grieving the death of a military or veteran loved one.

Wounded Warrior Project – www.WoundedWarriorProject.org

Camaraderie, peer support and grief groups, as well as other services for U.S. Veterans returning from conflict.

▶ **Writing workshops**
Corporeal Writing – www.corporealwriting.com
You're Going to Die – www.YG2D.com

Podcasts

There are so many listens, about grief, loss, connection, and education . . . Drop "grief" into your favorite podcast platform search bar and find specific grief-centered episodes, such as:

- "Grief and Holding Space for the Grieving," *Spirit School*, with Danielle Searancke
- "Time Traveling to Befriend Grief," *Labor of Love: A Podcast for BIPOC Adoptees Navigating Parenthood*
- "Invitation to Conscious Grieving," Claire Bidwell Smith featured on *Grief Is A Sneaky Bitch*, with Lisa Keefauver, MSW
- "Navigating Grief and the Afterlife with Mark Ireland," on *Grief 2 Growth*, with Brian Smith

Or, follow podcasts dedicated to talking about grief, support, and my favorite, metaphysics. These are a mix:

- *Grief Out Loud*, by the Dougy Center
- *griefsense*, with Mimi Gonzales
- *Dead Talks*, with David Ferrugio
- *Messages of Hope*, with Suzanne Giesemann
- *Coffee, Grief, and Gratitude,* with Anne Gudger and Maria Gibson

Social Media Channels

My go-to is Instagram. Follow the hashtags on your channels of choice to find more voices talking about grief and connection. Visit *@Ash.and.Spirit* to add your favorite resources for connecting (www.instagram.com/ash.and.spirit/).

On Instagram

- *@911Memorial* – News & highlights from the National September 11 Memorial Museum
- *@andreagibson* – Colorado poet laureate
- *@Ash.and.Spirit* – Add your resources to our IG channel
- *@BIPOCDeathGriefTalk* – Toronto-based collective care
- *@Dave.Markowitz* – Healing for Empaths, Sensitives, and Intuitives
- *@DrReneeLertzman* – Psychologist unlocking climate action with listening, presence and guiding
- *@FromGrieftoGrind* – A safe space for the forgotten grievers. Andrea A. Moore, Certified Life & Grief Coach, Bereaved Sibling Advocate
- *@GoodGriefNetwork* – Processing collective distress from climate trauma and systemic injustice. Redefining meaningful activism.
- *@GriefSense* – The Zillenial Griever. A safe space for creatives who are grievers, for us, by us.

- *@Let'sReimagine* – Transform the hard things in life to meaningful action and growth
- *@Only7Seconds* – Challenging you to fight loneliness by connecting with people in your life
- *@OptionB* – Navigating Grief and Hardship
- *@QueerGriefClub* – Queer Death Doula, End-of-Life Educator. Grief meetups and community.
- *@the_art_of_the_end* – Neurodivergent, inclusive support, planning, existential café space
- *@the.death.empath* – Alchemizing grief, death, loss of Self through Dance, Singing, Community Care
- *@TheDinnerParty* – A platform for grieving young adults to find peer community and build lasting relationships. Pull up a chair. Nonprofit organization.
- *@TheGriefCocoon* – Creative resources, workshops and community for grieving hearts
- *@UnlikelyCollaborators* – We help people understand others and their place in this (beautiful, batshit) world by untangling who we are beneath our stories.

Apps & Interactive

▶ **Self-Help Bereavement Guide**
www.nhsinform.scot/illnesses-and-conditions/mental-health
/mental-health-self-help-guides/bereavement-and-grief-self
-help-guide/

Scotland's National Health Service has incorporated elements of Cognitive Behavioral Therapy into an online self-help guide "for coping with bereavement and grief."

▶ **Transverse: A Divination Deck to Respond to Grief and Loss**
www.michellecjohnson.com

"A deck of cards accompanied by a booklet of descriptions and mantras to assist people in healing as they move through the process of grief," by author, Michelle C. Johnson.

▶ **Untangle Grief**
untanglegrief.com

Mobile app and community – "Holds your hand through all the emotional and logistical challenges that come after a bereavement, making it easier to rebuild your life."

Books

These books are but a few on grief (and some on listening and spirit), many of them suggested by community members in different forums I follow. Thanks to *@latinarebels* on Instagram and *Coffee & Grief* on Facebook for asking the hard questions and offering the vulnerability to receive several of these suggestions.

- Chimamanda Ngozi Adichie – *Notes on Grief*
- Joanne Cacciatore – *Bearing the Unbearable*

- Megan Devine – *It's Okay that You're Not Okay*
- Hope Edelman – *Motherless Daughters*
- Suzanne Giesemann – *Messages of Hope*
- Natalie Y. Gutiérrez – *The Pain We Carry: Healing from Complex PTSD for People of Color (The Social Justice Handbook Series)*
- Chenxing Han – *one long listening: a memoir of grief, friendship, and spiritual care*
- Laraine Herring – *The Grief Forest: a book about what we don't talk about*
- David Kessler – *Finding Meaning: The Sixth Stage of Grief* (Grief.com)
- Marisa Renee Lee – *Grief is Love: Living with Loss*
- Menakem, Resmaa – *My Grandmother's Hands*
- Leah Mele-Bazaz – *LAILA: Held for A Moment: A Memoir*
- Cindy Milstein (editor) – *Rebellious Mourning: The Collective Work of Grief*
- Martin Prechtel – *Grief and Praise: The Smell of Rain on Dust*
- Laura Seftel – *Grief Unseen: Healing Pregnancy Loss through the Arts*
- Christie Tate – *B.F.F: A Memoir of Friendship Lost and Found*
- Francis Weller – *The Wild Edge of Sorrow: Rituals of Renewal and the Sacred Work of Grief*

Guides

▶ **How to recognize grief in self and others**
www.betterup.com/blog/symptoms-of-grief

BetterUp.com is a virtual coaching platform used by organizations and companies to support their teams' mental health and personal and professional growth. Their blog is stocked with helpful guides on how to recognize grief, and ways to process it.

▶ **HelpGuide.org**
www.helpguide.org/articles/grief/helping-someone-who-is
-grieving.htm

A nonprofit and website established to support mental health and wellness. This link offers a guide on what to say and how to be present with someone who is grieving.

▶ **How to host an online grief circle**
www.thecircleway.net/booklets
The Circle Way Hosting Guide for Online Grief Circles

Areas of grief to explore

It's an ongoing wonder how grief shows up and when. Noticing it and allowing it to pass through has given me compassion for self and others, and has made me feel closer to the world around me.

Loss is felt from obvious blows, like death and traumas both old and new. But unspoken and unseen grief can exist as a daily hum in the background for some folks, and can include losses like separation, moves across the neighborhood or the globe, economic instability, geologic detriment, wars, silence, violence, oppression, microaggressions, power struggle, ego death, racism, shame, growing-pains of anti-racism work, labor over the same, neighborhoods degrading, neighborhoods growing, gentrification, climate change, missed opportunities, body dysmorphia, self-deprecation, loneliness, breakups, lost love . . .

. . . experienced by caregivers, loved ones, colleagues unknown to family members, teachers who have lost students, friends, entire groups hemmed in by systemic oppression, secret lovers, pet parents, children, friends, classmates, fans of celebrities and influencers, people of all faiths, nonbelievers, curmudgeons, open hearts, survivors, global empaths, activists . . .

I'm hoping that my incessant listing offers the reminder that we never know, deeply, really, who we're talking to and all they've experienced. But we can probably depend on the likelihood there has been loss in their lives. That's something we can relate on, and give each other a little space and listening for.

Printed in the USA
CPSIA information can be obtained
at www.ICGtesting.com
LVHW021542060924
790062LV00010B/48

9 781736 589885